E3

D1422814

REGIONAL ARCHAEOLOGIES   EDINBURGH AND SOUTH-EAST SCOTLAND

Fig. 1 Map of Mesolithic remains, Neolithic Long Cairns and Chambered Cairns

REGIONAL ARCHAEOLOGIES

Edinburgh and South-East Scotland

BY J. N. G. AND A. RITCHIE

HEINEMANN EDUCATIONAL BOOKS · LONDON

Regional Archaeologies

GENERAL EDITOR: D. M. WILSON, M.A., F.S.A.
*Professor of Medieval Archaeology
in the University of London*

Heinemann Educational Books Ltd
LONDON EDINBURGH MELBOURNE TORONTO
AUCKLAND SINGAPORE JOHANNESBURG KUALA LUMPUR
HONG KONG NAIROBI IBADAN NEW DELHI

ISBN 0 435 32971 5

© J. N. G. and A. Ritchie 1972
First published 1972

Published by Heinemann Educational Books Ltd
48 Charles Street, London W1X 8AH
Printed in Great Britain
by C. Tinling & Co. Ltd, London & Prescot

Contents

List of Illustrations

Acknowledgements

The authors wish to acknowledge their gratitude to friends and colleagues in the Royal Commission on the Ancient and Historical Monuments of Scotland and the National Museum of Antiquities of Scotland for their help in the preparation of this volume; particular thanks are also due to Dr. D. J. Breeze, Mr. D. V. Clarke, Mr. H. Pálsson, Professor S. Piggott and Mr. W. F. Ritchie. The Royal Scottish Academy has permitted publication of the axe from Cunzierton (fig. 9); the Department of the Environment has allowed mention in advance of publication of the site at Balbirnie excavated by the writers in 1970; Dr. J. M. Coles has generously allowed mention of the site at Morton Mains before publication; Messrs. Heinemann Ltd. have permitted the use of quotations from the Loeb translations; Mrs. Eva Wilson has redrawn the line illustrations. The authors wish also to acknowledge their debt to the many scholars and institutions whose original work has been consulted during the writing of this book.

The authors are indebted to the following individuals and organisations for permission to reproduce or adapt illustrations: University Museum of Archaeology and Ethnology, Cambridge (fig. 16); Crown Copyright, Department of the Environment (fig. 15); Miss A. S. Henshall (figs. 4, 5, 11, 12); Miss I. J. McInnes (figs. 6, 11); Crown Copyright, National Museum of Antiquities of Scotland (figs. 3, 8, 9, 14, 21, 24, 25, 33, 34, 36, 43, 46, 47); Professor S. Piggott (figs. 10, 16); Crown Copyright, Royal Commission on Ancient Monuments, Scotland (figs. 7, 13, 22, 23, 26, 27, 30, 35, 37, 38, 40); Crown Copyright, Dr. J. K. St Joseph, University of Cambridge, Air Photograph Library (figs. 42, 48); Society of Antiquaries of Scotland (figs. 3, 4, 10, 11, 16, 17, 28, 31, 32, 38, 39, 49).

Introduction

The region covered by this volume is divided into two main areas by the Firth of Forth. To the south of the Firth there are the coastal counties of the Lothians and Berwickshire, and from Berwick, following the river Tweed inland are the counties of Roxburgh, Selkirk and Peebles. The broad coastal plain of the Forth and the valley of the lower Tweed are rich agricultural land, with the bare massifs of the Moorfoot and Lammermuir Hills between them. To the south of the Rivers Tweed and Teviot, the Cheviot Hills form the line of the Border and the boundary of our region. North of the Firth of Forth and inland along the river the counties of Fife, Kinross, Clackmannan and Stirling form the northern part of the area. Some sites and finds, however, in southern Perthshire and Angus will also be included where relevant. The region, apart from the southern tip of Roxburghshire and the Loch Lomondside part of Stirlingshire, is covered by the Ordnance Survey Quarter Inch sheet, *The Firth of Forth*; the western boundary coincides with that of the companion volume, *South-West Scotland.*

GEOGRAPHY AND GEOLOGY

The region is divided geologically by the Southern Upland Fault, which separates the undulating lowland area of the Midland Valley from the uplands of southern Scotland. The major part of the Midland Valley is composed of sandstones and limestones belonging to the Old Red Sandstone and Carboniferous formations, while most of the Southern Uplands consist of Ordovician and Silurian greywackes and shales. Ice-movement during the Glacial Period resulted in the deposition of boulder clay in river valleys and over most of the Midland Valley. The soils which developed on these layers of boulder clay were particularly suited to the growth of woodland, thus providing a supply of timber which was exploited in prehistoric times by the builders of timber-laced forts and palisaded sites. Changes in sea-level, particularly after the ice had retreated, are apparent in the 'raised beaches' or old shore-lines visible along the coast of south-east Scotland, notably in the Forth-Tay area.

The region has a long and now very fertile coastal strip from the East Neuk of Fife to Dunbar, but the earliest settlement was concentrated not here but in the river valleys of the Forth and Tweed and on the seaside links and dunes of Tentsmuir (Fife) and between Gullane and Dunbar (East Lothian).

1 5000-3000 B.C.: Hunters and Gatherers

In the years between 5000 and 3000 B.C., when the climate was relatively warm and damp, much of southern Scotland was covered by forests of oak and mixed deciduous trees. The forest animals, including deer, wolf, bear and boar, provided much of the raw materials in the form of food and skins for the clothing of the small groups of hunters who were the first inhabitants of south Scotland. These hunters made their way northwards from Yorkshire and north-east England, following the coast of the Forth and the valley of the Tweed rather than striking into the more heavily afforested interior.

Two groups of hunters and gatherers in south-east Scotland can be detected by their different types of tools. In the valley of the Tweed, finds of small flint tools show one area of settlement indicating the activities of one group, while in the valley of the Forth a gathering and collecting way of life may be inferred from the large heaps of shells and the discovery of antler mattocks in the skeletons of stranded whales (fig. 1).

TWEED VALLEY

Our evidence for the hunters in the Tweed Valley comes entirely from chance finds of their stone and flint tools, mainly between Kelso and Peebles. The earliest hunters probably did not settle at once but made seasonal trips from north-east England to the untapped lowland forests. There is no reason to suppose that the Tweed was less attractive then as a fishing river than it is now. Concentrations of flint implements have been found in the 'haugh lands', the former flood plain of the Tweed, and on terraces near the river. The best known areas are Dryburgh Mains Farm (Berwickshire) and at Rink Farm (Selkirkshire).

Nodules and cores of flint are worked into shape by knocking off flake after flake until the required shape, a sharp point, a knife or a scraper, is achieved. Like a sculptor chipping at a block of stone to create a figure, the flint knapper leaves a vast amount of unwanted chips of flint round him as he works. Working sites can thus be seen as areas of discarded flint flakes, sometimes with unsuccessful or broken tools and abandoned cores. At Dryburgh Mains and Rink Farm such scatters of discarded flakes have been found, as well as examples of the completed tools themselves (fig. 2). Rink Farm is at the junction of the Rivers Ettrick and Tweed, and it is possible to think of it as a key area where hunting parties made expeditions along both rivers. There are two broad groups of such flint implements, namely those which are pointed and might be used to tip spears and throwing-darts for hunting (fig. 2) and those with longer cutting or scraping surfaces. The latter might be used to cut up and prepare the carcasses of animals for food, and also for scraping skins and pelts for use as clothing. Very few of these flint implements have been found north of the Tweed valley though isolated examples have been discovered at Hedderwick (East Lothian) and on the Meadows in Edinburgh. Several small flints have been found on hill-top sites in or near Edinburgh, for example on Arthur's

Seat and on Kaimes Hill, and these may show the presence of hunting parties from the Tweed or from the Tentsmuir area of Fife. Rather than continue round the coast, some groups of the Tweedside hunters made their way through the natural corridor between Peebles and Biggar and settled in the central part of the Clyde valley. Very small groups of people living by fishing, hunting and collecting berries and fruit should be envisaged. They probably followed the seasonal movements of the wild life which was their staple diet, and they would not build up any extensive communities or settlements.

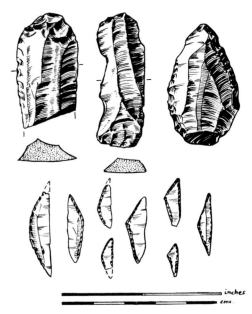

Fig. 2 Mesolithic implements from Tweedside

FORTH VALLEY

The shell-fish diet of similar groups in the upper valley of the Forth and the large mounds of discarded shells may suggest a more settled form of existence. The shell heap at Polmonthill (Stirlingshire), for example, measured about 75 by 500 ft in extent and was said to be between 2 to 3 ft thick. Other such middens have been found at Mumrills and Inveravon (Stirlingshire) and perhaps on the Island of Inchkeith in the Firth of Forth. The shells represented at Polmonthill included oysters, mussels, winkles, cockles and whelks. There were traces of fires and hearths in amongst the shell debris, suggesting perhaps that not all were eaten raw. It has been estimated that the waste shells of such a diet would accumulate at the rate of half a cubic foot per head per day. A midden the size of Polmonthill might thus represent the accumulated shells of about ten people over a period of some fifteen years of permanent occupation, or perhaps four times as long if it is seen as only seasonal occupation. No dateable artefacts have been found in these heaps to afford any indication of when this occupation took place.

STRANDED WHALES

The remains of stranded whales have been found in the upper valley of the Forth between Grangemouth and Cardross (fig. 1). At least seventeen whales have been recorded, with concentrations in the areas of Dunmore and Stirling. That the mesolithic communities made full use of these stranded sources of food is shown by antler tools found in the carcasses. These mattock-like implements are made of red-deer antler and are perforated to take a handle (cf fig. 3). They would be used for removing blubber and flesh from the stranded whales. The antler mattock-heads from Blair Drummond and Meiklewood still held the remains of their wooden handles.

Several dug-out canoes have been discovered embedded beneath deposits in the Carron and Forth valleys and, although there is no evidence of their date, some probably belonged to mesolithic communities. One boat, certainly dated to this general period and

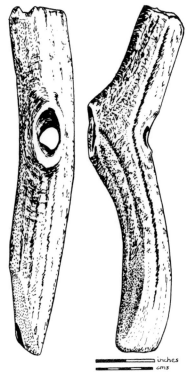

Fig. 3 Antler mattock-head from Meiklewood (Stirlingshire)

possibly to the sixth millennium B.C., came from Friarton near Perth and was found under a deposit of clay some 10 ft thick. The dug-out was 15 ft in length and had been hewn from a length of pine.

MORTON FARM

Recent excavations at Morton Farm on Tentsmuir have provided exciting new information about the way of life at this time. For the first time in this area huts with hearths, a midden and a chipping floor have been discovered together. The whole complex has been dated by the radiocarbon method to between 5400 and 4400 B.C. This method relies upon estimation of the rate of radio-active decay in natural substances and provides a period of time during which an event, such as the occupation of a site or the construction of a burial mound, is likely to have taken place. The Morton Farm site lies on a slight rise amongst the sand dunes; the various archaeological levels were separated by layers of wind-blown sand, indicating that there was probably only intermittent occupation. The huts are up to 8 ft in diameter and were probably built with a framework of supple branches perhaps covered by skins. The scattered remains of tiny waste flint flakes show that tools were made on the spot, and some were made from hard semi-precious stones including agate and chalcedony. The midden deposit showed that, as for the mesolithic people in the Forth valley, shell fish were an important source of food, and that fish and seabirds provided additional items in their diet.

This period of prehistory in south-east Scotland is thus characterised by small bands of hunters moving along the Tweed valley, setting up small hunting-camps and, when necessary, working-places to make new flint implements. Other groups of hunters, with greater dependence on shell fish as a source of food, lived in the Forth valley.

2 3000-2000 B.C.: The First Farmers

The development of settled farming communities in lowland Scotland took place during the third millennium B.C. as a result of the arrival of new settlers, probably in small bands, from eastern England and the Irish Sea zone. This colonisation was taking place over much of Britain, and, since surviving traces of these settlers are few in south-east Scotland, most of our information about them is derived from evidence found elsewhere. These neolithic people are characterised by the introduction of a farming economy, the manufacture and use of pottery and the construction of elaborate funerary monuments, and their way of life was in complete contrast to that of the groups of hunters before them. Instead of being nomadic and following their sources of food, the new farmers formed settled communities based on food production rather than food gathering. This contrast might be compared to the situation in central America when buffalo-hunting Indian tribes were confronted by the European settlers.

The farming economy included both agriculture and stock-rearing; although in some regions, including south-east Scotland, the stock-raising element was probably predominant. Areas such as East Lothian and Berwickshire are rich agricultural counties today, but they were not immediately attractive to these early farmers whose primitive methods and technology were unsuited to the heavy soils and thick tree-cover. If agriculture was practised in this area, it would have taken the form of small plots won from the forest by burning down a small patch of thin trees and scrub and planting the precious seed in the ash which acted as a fertiliser. When a series of such fields was exhausted, a further area would be cleared in the same way. For fodder in the winter months, when only a small number of animals would be kept, branches of trees, particularly elm, were probably collected and gathered into bunches for the stock.

The development of this type of economy had an important effect upon society, for food production and storage allowed an increase in population and even provided a surplus of labour which could be utilised for the construction of elaborate tombs. It is difficult to imagine the importance to these peasant farmers of their funerary monuments, yet it is these that provide their most impressive testimony in the archaeological record. In the north and west of Scotland, they built large stone burial-chambers enclosed within sub-

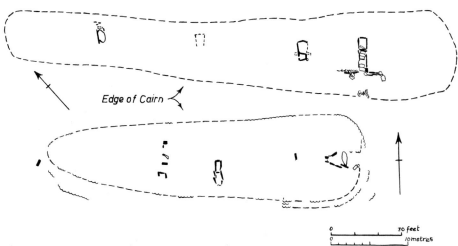

Fig. 4 Chambered Cairns, Clach na Tiompan and Kindrochat (Perthshire)

13

stantial cairns of stone, and the major areas of neolithic settlement can be discovered from the distribution of such chambered cairns. Only in Perthshire, Stirlingshire and in Lanarkshire, on the borders of our area, are there groups of such cairns, and these are presumably offshoots from the Clyde region. There are, however, a few long cairns which must belong to this period, partly because of their similarity to earthen long mounds in east and south-east England, and partly because the building of elongated mounds of stones appears to be connected with chambered tomb traditions.

LONG CAIRNS

The most striking example of a long cairn, The Mutiny Stones, stands in moorland west-north-west of Longformacus (Berwickshire) and is almost 280 ft in length. Excavation at the north-eastern end of the cairn in 1924, when it still stood to a height of almost 12 ft, laid bare a stretch of dry-stone walling, but there were no signs of a burial chamber.

Of two sites in Roxburghshire, Caverton Hillhead and the Long Knowe, the former is known only from an early description which gives it a length of 342 ft and a breadth between 27 ft and 42 ft. The Long Knowe, which is situated in the extreme south of the region, is 175 ft long and up to 45 ft broad. In the south-west there are further examples of rather more compact long cairns in Dumfriesshire and Kirkcudbrightshire. The long cairn on Harlaw Muir (Peeblesshire) is now a very ruined mound of stones aligned north-east/south-west, measuring about 190 ft in length. The considerable heights at which these cairns have been found – 1250 ft, 930 ft and 890 ft above sea level, for the Mutiny Stones, Harlaw Muir and the Long Knowe respectively – suggest that the early agriculturists were in some cases at least avoiding the thicker woodland and the heavier soils of the valleys, and that some communities were leading a mainly pastoral life in the uplands. The exception is the destroyed site at Caverton Hillhead, which is a reminder that some long barrows may have been destroyed or ploughed out in the more intensively cultivated areas.

CHAMBERED CAIRNS

It has been suggested that the builders of chambered cairns for collective burial, the first agriculturalists in the western part of our area, made their way up the Clyde into south Dunbartonshire and south-west Stirlingshire. Instead of continuing eastwards across the Clyde-Forth isthmus, they seem to have moved either up Loch Lomond and thence across Loch Voil to Loch Earn, or up Loch Fyne and across to Tayside. Perhaps the thick oak forest which then blanketed the valley of the Forth above Stirling formed a barrier to their advance in this direction. One cairn at Burngrange on the Westruther Burn (Lanarkshire) shows that some of the settlers found their way probably up the Clyde to the foothills of the Pentlands.

In west Stirlingshire and in Strathearn there are chambered cairns which were used for burials over a long period of time, rather in the manner of family burial-vaults. There are impressive remains at Clach na Tiompan in Glen Almond, Kindrochat, Rottenreoch and Cultoquhey in Strathearn. The simplest chamber is that at Cultoquhey, which consists of six slabs forming a rectangular box-like structure inserted into the edge of a largely natural mound and divided into two by a cross-slab. The chamber would be covered by flat capstones. Excavation showed that the final burial was an inhumation which was accompanied by a leaf-shaped flint arrowhead. Sherds of a round-based pot with lugs for suspension were also discovered. A similar arrowhead was the

Fig. 5   Clach na Tiompan (Perthshire), blocking of SE chamber

only find from the cairn at Kindrochat, a long mound of boulders which contained three chambers, two at right angles to the long axis of the cairn and one at right angles to a short side at the east end (fig. 4).

At Clach na Tiompan there is also an impressive mound of stones, in which four chambers are known to have existed (fig. 4). The south-east chamber at Clach na Tiompan is perhaps the most complete and best excavated example. The chamber measured 12 ft 3 in. in length, up to 3 ft 3 in. broad and was divided by upright slabs into three compartments which would probably have been rather more than 3 ft in height. The floor of the chamber would have been paved with flat slabs. Burials would be placed in these compartments and the entrance then sealed with dry-stone walling (fig. 5); later burials might then be inserted by removing the walling and pushing aside the older bodies. Along with the burials, deposits of pottery, perhaps containing offerings of food, were often placed in the tombs. Another long cairn at Aucheneck on Stockie Muir in Stirlingshire measures about 60 ft long; the remains of a straight-sided chamber can still be seen in the cairn material, but it is too ruined to interpret completely.

In summary, Neolithic chambered cairns were designed for collective burial rather than for the interment of a single person, and the building of the cairns was an expression of faith or respect by a settled community. The effort involved in constructing these tombs would indicate that a larger number of people helped in the building than were eventually buried within them. We are therefore dealing with a form of social stratification, and we should envisage the burials as those of special people, social or religious leaders of the time.

POTTERY

Although we know nothing of the houses or

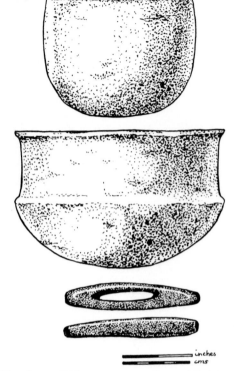

Fig. 6 Neolithic pottery; Roslin (Midlothian), Clatchard Craig (Fife); Jet slider; Balgone (East Lothian)

farms of these people, some examples of their pottery and flint tools have survived from south-east Scotland. Unlike their predecessors, whose containers must have been made of bone, wood or skins, these farmers had brought with them the knowledge of how to make and fire pottery vessels. The earliest types of pottery, dating to about the beginning of the 3rd millennium B.C., have affinities with vessels in Yorkshire. They are gracefully shouldered bowls with a concave neck. Simple bowls have also been found like one from Roslin, Midlothian (fig. 6), which has a distinct rim, possibly so that a cord could be tied round it. Vessels which are thought to be related to an Irish type of pottery known as Lyles Hill ware have been found on Clatchard Craig, in Fife (fig. 6) and in the Clyde type chambered cairn at Cultoquhey (Perthshire); these date to rather later in the 3rd millennium. Although it may seem surprising to speak of such wide-ranging connections for the pottery of this date, when we come to examine the stone axes of this period it will become clear that such contacts were certainly made, either through local trade or through the movement either of groups of people or of individual merchants.

It is in the areas of sand dunes near Tentsmuir in Fife and near Gullane and North Berwick in East Lothian that deposits of rubbish in the form of pottery and bone provide the best evidence of habitation sites dating to about the end of the 3rd millennium B.C. The sand dunes were settled not only because of the ease with which small boats could be beached but also because small patches of crops could be easily cultivated in the light sandy soil.

STONE AXES

The third millennium, the period in south-east Scotland of the first farmers, has also been called the Neolithic or New Stone Age, because cutting and scraping tools were made of stone and flint and the working of metal was unknown. The choice of suitable stone for making axes was very important, for it needed to be a type which would not fracture easily while being worked (fig. 7). One of the most remarkable illustrations of the economy of the neolithic period is the distance over which suitable stone and axes were traded; in southeast Scotland, axes have been discovered which are made of stone that occurs naturally at Great Langdale (Westmorland), Tievebulliagh and Rathlin Island (Co. Antrim) and Graig Lwyd in North Wales. Smaller tools,

Fig. 7 Polished stone axes from Peeblesshire

17

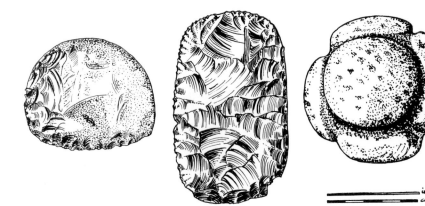

Fig. 8 Stone and flint implements of the third millennium; flint knives, Bonchester Bridge (Roxburghshire), Butterlaw (Berwickshire); Carved stone ball, Newburgh (Fife)

particularly scrapers, have in a few cases been made from pitchstone which comes from near Brodick on Arran.

Axes from the Langdale area of the Lake District have been found at Cornhill-on-Tweed and Preston (Berwickshire), Hownam Rings (Roxburghshire), Ashybank (Selkirkshire) and Denny (Stirlingshire). Radiocarbon dating outside this area suggests a date between about 2500 and 2000 B.C. for the exploitation of this type of rock. Graig Lwyd stone is uncommon in south-east Scotland, but a fragment of an axe of this type has been found at the sanctuary site of Cairnpapple (West Lothian), along with Langdale stone. This suggests that the users of the site had contact, however indirect, with the 'axe factories' of the Irish Sea zone. The fragments were probably, though not certainly, associated with the first phase on this site, a cremation cemetery with 'ritual' pits. The two ceremonial jadeite axes from Cunzierton in Roxburghshire (fig. 9) and similar axes from Stirling, Dunfermline and Greenlaw represent a later type which indicates even more far-reaching connections. The most likely origin for this type of stone is the German Rhineland, and the axes were probably introduced by the makers of Beaker pottery from this

area. A fragment was found in the blocking of the chambered tomb at Cairnholy I (Kirkcudbrightshire) and was associated with late Neolithic impressed ware and Beaker pottery.

During the third millennium three main flint tools were used – 'leaf-shaped' arrowheads, long and polished knives, and knives with a rounded cutting or scraping edge (fig. 8). From a study of the leaf-shaped arrowheads, it has been shown that the Lothians and the Tay and Forth Basins were only sparsely populated compared to north-east Scotland, thus supporting the impression already noted from the scarcity of surviving monuments. The number of such arrowheads increases in the Tweed Basin where there are also examples of flint knives. Other objects of later 3rd and early 2nd millennium date in south-east Scotland include lopsided flint arrowheads and a single example of a jet 'belt fastener' or 'slider' (fig. 6). Carved stone balls and maceheads (fig. 8) seem to belong to this period, although few have been found with any helpful association; their distribution lies predominantly in north-east Scotland, but several have been found in the south-east, notably a concentration of carved stone balls in northern Fife. These small and skilfully decorated balls are unique to

18

Scotland and their purpose is unknown. Perhaps they formed part of a game, perhaps they have a much more serious religious function. The beautifully-made perforated stone maceheads may have been ceremonial objects or just possibly actual weapons. At Glenhead Farm, Doune (Perthshire), a pestle macehead was found in a cist under a cairn, together with a Food Vessel belonging to the mid-2nd millennium B.C.

Fig. 9 Jadeite axes, Cunzierton (Roxburghshire)

3 2000-600 B.C.: The First Metal-Workers

The apparent sparseness of neolithic occupation in south-east Scotland may be contrasted to the increase of activity in the area in the 2nd and 1st millennia. The archaeological information is very one-sided, and, although there is a mass of information about burial and ritual sites, nothing is known about the houses or farms of this period. Much of the pottery discovered was interred with a burial deposit either as a grave offering or, particularly in the case of Cinerary Urns, actually containing the remains. During this period the ability to work with metals became widespread, and objects of bronze and gold are found. As the 2nd millennium progressed, the number of objects and the degree of competence of their craftsmanship may be seen to increase. This chapter is divided into three sections – the first dealing with burial sites and associated pottery, the second with other visible monuments such as standing stones, cairns and cup-marked-stones, and the third with bronze working.

CAIRNPAPPLE

The important excavation at Cairnpapple Hill (West Lothian) provides a sequence of ritual and burial ideas in the first half of the second millennium B.C. This complex site occupies the summit of Cairnpapple Hill about fifteen miles west of Edinburgh; from the hill-top there is an outstanding view across the Lothians and the Firth of Forth. Like the Balbirnie area of Fife, Cairnpapple was an important religious centre over a period of about six centuries, illustrating the changing burial and pottery traditions from about 2000 B.C. to approximately 1400 B.C. Five distinct periods were recognised (fig. 10), beginning with a cremation cemetery (1). This was followed by the construction of a ceremonial site of a type known as a henge monument, consisting of a sub-circular bank with an internal quarry ditch and two opposed entrances. An oval setting of twenty-four standing stones was erected within the ditch and bank, and two burials were made, each possessing complete pottery vessels of Beaker type (2). In the third period of activity on the site, the oval of standing stones was taken down and a cairn, 50 ft in diameter, was built to cover two stone cists, one containing a pot of Food Vessel type (3). This cairn was subsequently enlarged to twice its original diameter, and covered two Cinerary

Urns each set upside down over a cremated burial (4). The final period is represented by four undatable inhumation burials with the skeletons laid out in extended position (5).

We shall consider here the types of monument illustrated by the first four chronological phases at Cairnpapple, so that the Cairnpapple sequence may be related to similar sites in south-east Scotland.

CREMATION CEMETERIES (Cairnpapple 1)

Period I at Cairnpapple appears to have been unique in this region; it consisted of seven small pits, six of which contained deposits of cremated human bone and a filling of stone rubble. A small bone or antler pin was found with a cremation in one of the holes, and this pin provides the best evidence of the date of these ritual pits and of a setting of three stone holes which seemed to be associated with them. This period of activity may date to approximately 2000 B.C. A pit, which may be compared to those of Cairnpapple I, was found at Brackmont Mill (Fife); it measured 4 ft in diameter and 3 ft 2 in. deep, and in it were found fragments of at least twenty Late Neolithic vessels. Over half of the sherds belonged to the rims of pots, and it is an interesting possibility that the pots may have been broken after a funeral feast, although no actual burial remains were discovered.

HENGE MONUMENTS (Cairnpapple 2)

Henge monuments are circular or oval ritual enclosures formed by an exterior bank and an internal quarry ditch. Two classes of henge have been distinguished, depending on the number of entrances through the bank and ditch. The earlier type, with only one entrance, is represented by two sites in south-east Scotland, at Balfarg (Fife) and Overhowden (Berwickshire), but both have now been ploughed almost flat. These·henges, which measure 300 ft and 325 ft respectively, were discovered

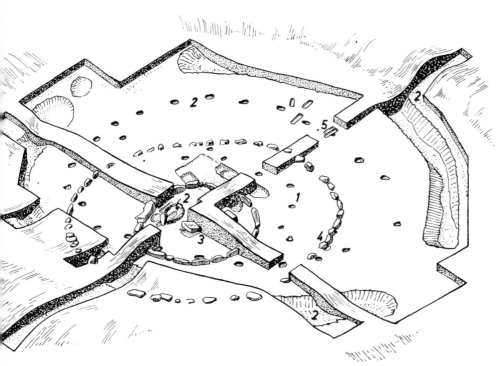

Fig. 10 Isometric plan of Cairnpapple (West Lothian); numbers indicate structural sequence.

during the scanning of air photographs and there is very little to be seen on the ground. Two large standing stones mark the south side of the entrance at Balfarg, one inside the henge and the other outside it, and it is possible that there once existed a complete inner circle comparable to that at Cairnpapple. There are no datable finds directly associated with either of these henges but, in the vicinity of Over-howden, several arrowheads, scrapers and a polished mace-head, all characteristic of the later Neolithic period, have been discovered. It is difficult to suggest a purpose for these earthworks, but it is likely that they formed a focus for acts of ritual or worship. Had the bank formed 'terraces' for spectators, as has sometimes been suggested, it is perhaps likely that more debris or 'litter' would have been

found in the filled ditch.

The later type of henge has two opposing entrances through the bank and ditch and this type, which is often associated with Beaker pottery and burials, is represented by the second phase at Cairnpapple Hill. A circle of twenty-four standing stones originally existed on the inner edge of the ditch of the henge at Cairnpapple. In the centre of the henge, a series of pits forming a rectangular setting was found. The function of these pits is difficult to explain, but they may represent the sole re-maining traces of a rectangular setting of stones, the holes having been left when the stones were removed. This interpretation is suggested by surviving examples of such stone settings at Balbirnie (Fife) and Mount Pleasant (Dorset). On the west side of the Cairnpapple henge, there was an unusual burial accompanied by pottery vessels of Beaker type. The burial was placed in a rock-cut grave surrounded by a setting of ten stones, and an impressive slab stood at its west end. The grave had probably been covered by a small cairn. An area of staining on the floor in the centre of the grave suggested the position of the body, a position confirmed by the presence of a number of teeth at one end of the stain. A patch of carbonised oak found above the teeth has been interpreted as the remains of some wooden object which had been placed over the face of the body as part of the burial ritual. A length of oak, 3 ft 6 in. long and about 3 inches in diameter, lay alongside the body and may have been a club.

BEAKER POTTERY

From the beginning of the 2nd millennium for about 300 years, east Scotland was subjected to a series of invasions from across the North Sea, from the Low Countries and the Rhineland. The reasons behind the invasions are not known, and the numbers of people involved were probably comparatively small. The intruders may be detected not only by their distinctive pottery vessels but also by their skull formation. The physical appearance of the makers of Beaker pottery is quite distinct from that of the builders of chambered tombs; the incomers seem, on the evidence of skeletons in cists, to have been slightly taller and, in general, of a heavier build than the native population. Their Beakers were finely made pots in thin well-fired reddish ware and may be divided on the basis of decoration into several distinct types. The earliest are those decorated over the complete outside surface with the horizontal impression of a two-strand cord (All-Over-Cord Beakers), and those decorated with a toothed comb in a wider range of motifs including bands of lattice work and pendant triangles (European Bell Beakers).

The makers of Beaker pottery introduced a new funerary rite which contrasted with the previous collective burials in long mounds and chambered tombs. The dead were deposited individually and in a crouched position in small stone-lined coffins, sometimes under cairns of boulders. In southern Britain Beaker burials were in pit graves, possibly in wooden coffins, under earthen barrows. In south-east Scotland All-Over-Cord decorated Beakers have been found at Bailielands, Auchterarder (Perthshire) and in the central cist of the cairn at Drumelzier (Peeblesshire). The discovery of Late Neolithic pottery in this latter cist (as well as a fragment of a second Beaker and a number of flints) suggests that the change in tradition was a gradual one.

COASTAL SETTLEMENTS

No houses belonging to the Beaker period have been found in south-east Scotland, but there are several important concentrations of pottery in sand dune sites. It is therefore likely that some of the Beaker people lived in small wooden huts nearby. All that survives in the sands of East Lothian, at Gullane, North Berwick and Dunbar, and at Tentsmuir in Fife, are the rubbish dumps or middens yielding Beakers, quantities of shells, animal bones and antler fragments.

Some few sherds show the impressions of grain but the shells and antler fragments indicate that, apart from agriculture, gathering food from the shore and hunting were also important to the economy. Some arrowheads have been found on sites with Beaker pottery of these two early types, but the bow does not seem to have been such an important weapon for these people as for later invaders. The flint work associated with Beaker pottery in East Lothian and Fife middens is essentially domestic and consists of scrapers and small knives as well as quantities of small flakes.

In the decades around 1700 B.C. further

Fig. 11 Beaker, arrowheads, awl, Springwood (Roxburghshire)

wood (Roxburghshire) contained an inhumation burial, a Beaker of Dutch derivation, five small flint arrowheads and a broken metal awl or piercing tool (fig. 11). The Beaker people, of this group at least, were thus archers and had some knowledge of metal-working, previously unknown in south-east Scotland. They did not slight the religious sites of the native population and sometimes shared in the use of existing sacred monuments – indeed such contact is perhaps the best evidence surviving of the intermingling of the two sets of people. A Beaker, with similarities to those in the North Rhine area, was found at Cairnpapple with a burial, possibly of a child; the burial had been placed beside one of the uprights of the standing stone circle.

LOCAL BEAKER GROUPS

Developing from these vessels which have a recognisable European ancestry was a series of Beakers with elaborate decorative motifs in a purely insular style. Many of these have been found in cist burials, particularly in East Lothian and Berwickshire; Beaker cists have also been found round the coastal strip and in the valleys of the Forth and Tweed. Often such cists are found casually when deeper ploughing dislodges a capstone under the earth. Several cairns have secondary burials inserted into an already existing cairn or barrow. At Collessie in Fife, in the centre of a 60 ft cairn, was a cist with a skeleton accompanied by a Beaker. A second Beaker rather later in style was found with a cremation burial in a pit some distance from the centre of the mound. At the edge of this cairn was another cremation burial in a pit with which there was a bronze riveted knife dagger with a gold-mounted hilt.

METAL OBJECTS

The use of metal had been increasing in south-east Scotland as the makers of Northern Beak-

bands of invaders landed on the shores of south-east Scotland from the Low Countries and the valley of the Rhine. Again they were makers of Beaker pottery in distinctive styles, and the Beakers found in cists in south-east Scotland are very similar to those discovered on the continent. The vessels are often taller than those of the earlier groups, with a graceful S-profile, and are decorated with bands of comb-impressed ornament. They have been found in cists with both inhumations in a crouched position, with the legs bent, and cremation burials. In a few cases the cists have been covered by small cairns or earthen barrows, and it is possible that other mounds may have been ploughed flat. Apart from pottery there are few finds associated with these burials to show what else they might have brought with them. A cist burial at Spring-

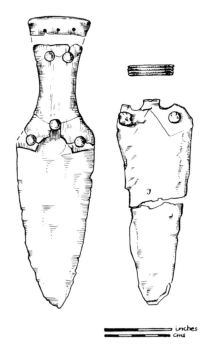

Fig. 12 Daggers; Ashgrove (Fife), Skateraw (East Lothian)

which contained bronze daggers, the earliest products of a developing bronze industry in the area. The Ashgrove cist contained a crouched burial associated with a scored Beaker and a fine bronze dagger with the remains of a leather sheath (fig. 12). The hilt of the dagger also survived and consisted of two horn hilt-plates surmounted by an ivory pommel, possibly made from the tooth of a sperm whale. The handle was attached to the blade by three sturdy bronze rivets. The skeleton was covered by an unusual mass of vegetable fibres including sphagnum moss, lime and meadow sweet, which might suggest that the moss was used as a surgical dressing, and that bunches of flowers were laid across the body. A dagger, with two rivets to attach it to a hilt, was found with another scored Beaker in a cist at Linlathen (Angus); a notable feature of this cist was the clay sealing its corners, presumably to keep the burial watertight. If the Ashgrove dagger provided information about the hilt of such weapons, a cist burial with a dagger at Kirkcaldy (found a few feet away from the cist containing the jet buttons discussed above) is almost unique in containing a small sheath. Two strips of horn formed the mouth, and sewn to these by thongs was the sheath itself with two layers of skin folded over and stretched down one side. We thus have a clearer picture of the warrior of the final Beaker groups than of earlier peoples, well-built, standing perhaps to a height of 5 ft 9 in, of broadish face and short skull, with a buttoned jacket and a small bronze dagger hanging in a skin sheath at his belt. Such daggers are rare and belong to the end of the period of use of Beaker pottery, about the 16th century B.C.

Four daggers probably date to the succeeding century on stylistic grounds; one, from a cairn at Collessie (Fife), had a pommel mounting of gold, but it was associated only with a cremation burial. A similar dagger with a gold

ers made their impact on the native population, but copper and bronze artefacts were still very rare and there are few direct associations with Beaker ware. Other Beakers suggest the arrival of people from Eastern England and these are characterised by incised or scored decoration. Three representative cist burials are those from Kirkcaldy and Ashgrove (Fife) and Linlathen (Angus). In the Kirkcaldy cist an inhumation was associated with a scored Beaker, a small tanged knife with a handle of hazel wood, a small copper or bronze awl and twelve buttons made of jet. Here we have one of the few hints of the form of clothing of the Beaker people for the buttons were probably sewn to the front of a closely-fitting jacket.

The burials from Ashgrove and Linlathen form a suitable introduction to an exciting series of warrior graves in south-east Scotland

pommel was found in a cist under a large cairn at Skateraw (East Lothian) which was destroyed in the early 19th century (fig. 12). A dagger from another clay-sealed cist in a cairn at Auchterhouse (Angus) had a horn hilt and a ribbed bronze blade, further decorated by lines of dots running down each side of the ribs. An unusually large cist from Masterton (Fife) was also sealed with clay and was covered by two very large capstones. The grave goods suggest that the cist had contained a double burial of a man and a woman. A dagger lay along one side of the cist and a small bronze blade, a pair of armlets and a jet necklace on the other side. The dagger was the prerogative of the warrior, while the small knife and the personal ornaments might perhaps have belonged to a woman.

GOLD LUNULAE and JET NECKLACES
Elaborate neck ornaments of gold known as lunulae and crescentic jet necklaces were in use during the first half of the second millennium B.C. The lunula is a crescent-shaped necklet of gold which has been beaten to a thin sheet of metal and often finely decorated on the upper surface. The majority of such finds come from north and west Ireland but, of the six Scottish examples, three have been found on the borders of our region; one is from Monzie, near Crieff (Perthshire), and two come from Southside Farm (Peeblesshire) (fig. 13). These last two superb pieces are decorated, perhaps by the same craftsman, with incised lines round the edges of the lunulae, and a series of punched dots at intervals round two of the lines. The origin of lunulae used to be sought in the decorative motifs of the crescentic necklaces of amber or jet, but it has recently been suggested that they may have been an independent invention in Ireland, borrowing motifs from Beaker pottery decoration and probably dating to about 1700 B.C. The simplest form of necklace made of jet beads

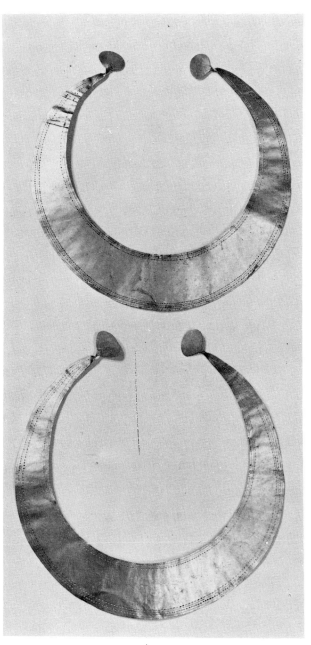

Fig. 13a Lunulae, Southside (Peeblesshire)

25

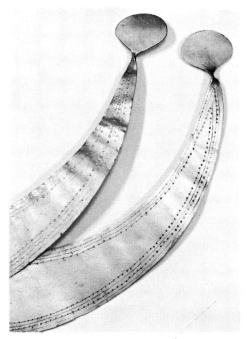

Fig. 13b Lunulae, Southside (Peeblesshire), details of terminals

consists of a single strand of small washer-like jet discs or of small barrel-shaped beads. A necklace consisting of sixty-four disc- and ten barrel-shaped beads has been found at Greenhill, Balmerino (Fife); in the cist already mentioned from Masterton, and in association with the dagger and armlets, a necklace of sixty-seven barrel beads and ninety-one disc beads was discovered. The position of these beads in the cist showed that they had been strung together as a necklace at the time of the burial and that the necklace comprised five strings of barrel-beads with disc beads at the ends. A triangular toggle at one end of the necklace would be threaded through a looped thong at the other as the means of fastening it (fig. 14).

Crescent-shaped necklaces were also made of jet beads, cleverly constructed so that the strings of beads were held in the formal crescent pattern. This was achieved by starting with four strands of beads, with a triangular bead at either end to act as terminals, then

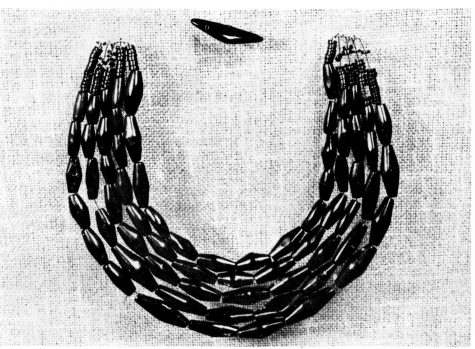

Fig. 14 Jet necklace, Masterton (Fife)

using two 'spacer' beads with complex perforations which allowed the number of strands to be increased to seven in the central section of the necklace. These spacer beads are sometimes decorated with dot designs in a way that echoes the pattern of the borings through the bead. Several of these necklaces, including that from Balgay, Tayfield (Fife), have been found in cists together with Food Vessels indicating that they were still in fashion around the fifteenth century B.C.

FOOD VESSELS

Two groups of pottery vessels take the place of Beakers in the burial deposits of the period about 1500 to 1100 B.C. – namely *Food Vessels* and *Cinerary Urns*. There was perhaps a shift of population westwards from one of the main areas of Beaker settlement in Berwickshire and East Lothian to Midlothian; the Cinerary Urn cemeteries of Magdalene Bridge and Musselburgh must indicate settled communities nearby. It is difficult to find a precise origin for these pottery styles, but they are certainly insular and do not represent invasions as did the Beaker vessels. It seems likely that Food Vessels are an amalgam of Late Neolithic and Beaker pottery styles. The principal types of Food Vessel found in southeast Scotland are: *Irish Bowls*, which include both smooth-profiled bowls and those which are divided by raised ridges into three zones, sometimes with impressed decoration on the ridges, *Irish Vase Food Vessels*, which are vase-shaped vessels normally with a pronounced shoulder and a rather narrow everted rim, and *Yorkshire Vase Food Vessels*, a similarly shaped jar with a distinct groove round the shoulder, with cord-impressed decoration and sometimes impressions made with a round-toothed comb. These vessels occur both with inhumation and cremation burials, thus bridging the change in burial custom from Beaker inhumation to Cinerary Urn cremation, but the predominance of inhumation stresses an early overlap with Beaker-making peoples.

Fig. 15   Food Vessel, Balbirnie (Fife)

27

The burials were normally placed in cists, sometimes in cist-groups or cemeteries and sometimes beneath mounds. The most common grave-goods associated with Food Vessels are beautifully made flint knives (known, from their shape, as plano-convex knives), and necklaces of jet and lignite beads.

CINERARY URNS

Cinerary Urns are rather larger vessels and, as their name suggests, were used to contain the ashes from cremation burials. Four main types of urn occur; *Collared Urns* have a thick collar or band round the rim; the outer surfaces of *Cordoned Urns* are decorated with two or three thinner horizontal ribs; *Encrusted Urns* are decorated with applied strips and bosses; *Enlarged Food Vessel* is an unsatisfactory residual category which covers urns of Food Vessel shape but of rather greater dimensions. It has sometimes been suggested that the collars, cordons and applied decoration of Cinerary Urns reflect techniques used for rope bindings and methods of suspension or sealing large domestic vessels. It is possible, particularly in the case of Encrusted Urns, the decoration of which seems to copy in clay the idea of rope binding, that these pots were made specifically for burial purposes and that they were not used in domestic life. Cinerary Urns were certainly in use during the second half of the second millennium – a radiocarbon sample from a Cordoned Urn from Grandtully (Perthshire) provided a date centred on 1270 B.C. – but, as with Food Vessels, it is not known precisely how long they continued in use. Cinerary Urns are often discovered in the course of gravel-digging or ploughing and, as they are without the protection of a cist, they are perhaps more liable to be recovered in a damaged condition than are Beakers or Food Vessels.

Small accessory vessels have been found associated with Urns, for example at Esperston

Fig. 16 Cinerary Urn, Cairnpapple (West Lothian); Accessory vessel, Esperston (Midlothian)

Lime Quarry, Gorebridge (Midlothian) (fig. 16). Small bronze blades or razors were deposited with the cremations at Brackmont Mill and Law Park (Fife), Shanwell (Kinross) and Magdalene Bridge in Edinburgh (fig. 17).

Cemeteries such as Brackmont Mill with its eighteen burials and Law Park with its twenty urns must have been in use over a considerable period of time; but the pits containing the urns are rarely found on top of, or cutting into, one another; this suggests that the position of the burials was marked in some way on the surface, perhaps by a small stone or a stick but certainly in a way that has left no trace.

CAIRNPAPPLE 3 and 4

In period 3 at Cairnpapple Hill, a stone cist (fig. 10) containing a Food Vessel formed the central burial within a cairn, 45 ft in diameter. The pot had been placed on a small shelf, and it accompanied an inhumation

28

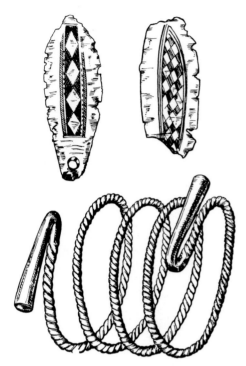

Fig. 17 Razors, Shanwell (Kinross-shire), Magdalene Bridge (Edinburgh); gold armlet, Slateford (Edinburgh)

burial. The cist also contained a stone bearing three cup-marks, a decorative feature discussed on p. 31. A second cist was found beneath the cairn, presumably contemporary with the other but yielding only a cremated burial.

The cairn, which completely enveloped the earlier Beaker grave, is situated on the highest point of the hill just within the henge monument, the ditch of which had begun to fill up with silt by this time. The cairn, however, overlay part of the line of the stone circle and all the stones had been removed leaving only the stone holes to be discovered in the course of excavation. The stones themselves were used on their sides to form an impressive kerb to the cairn.

Rather later in the 2nd millennium this cairn was enlarged to a diameter of 100 ft, and two Cinerary Urn burials were inserted in shallow pits (fig. 16); associated with these were two pins, one of red-deer antler and the other of bone. The effort required to build the enlargement to the cairn is in contrast to many Cinerary Urn burials which were inserted into existing cairns, into natural knolls, or into a hole in the ground.

CAIRNS

Some of the most impressive cairns are situated on the tops of hills, such as those on the summits of Spartleton and Harestone Hill (East Lothian) and the West Lomond (Fife) and on the ridges of the Cheviot foothills. These cairns were evidently intended to be visible from great distances, as expressions of piety or respect. Most burial cairns, however, were probably built closer to the settlements and farms of individual communities.

STANDING STONES

The possible reasons behind the erection of standing stones have exercised Scottish antiquaries for many years. Over eighty are still in position in south-east Scotland and many others have been recorded in the past but are now fallen or have been removed to facilitate cultivation. Several form small groups and others are associated with cairns, as at Newbridge (Midlothian). But in general very little is known about their purpose and date, although the majority probably belong to the second millennium B.C. Some may have marked boundaries between farms or communities, other may be meeting-places or route markers, and it has recently been suggested that some may have been used in studying the moon and stars. In many cases, however, we are probably justified in attributing a ritual significance to circles and linear settings of standing stones.

STONE CIRCLES

At least seventeen stone circles survive in a recognisable condition in our area, but it is evident that more existed at one time. There are early descriptions of stone circles now destroyed, as well as records of stones removed from settings such as those at Newbridge (Midlothian) and Lundin Links (Fife). An unusual type of circle is found in the south-east, the stones of which are much smaller than most normally associated with such structures. Examples of this group may be seen on Borrowstoun Rig (Berwickshire), where none of the stones is more than 2 ft in height, and on Kingside Hill (East Lothian), where there is an additional large boulder in the centre of the circle. There is an attractive small circle, with stones up to 4 ft in height, in a garden at Harestanes (Peeblesshire). In contrast, the three impressive stones at Lundin Links, which were originally part of a circle or setting of at least four stones, stand to heights of up to 18 ft.

COMPOSITE MONUMENTS

The site at Cairnpapple has been seen to consist of several structural elements of the second millennium B.C., elements which elsewhere occur separately. The site is thus a composite monument, the result of ritual and funerary activities over a long period of time. A comparable sequence of structures has been revealed by excavations at Balbirnie (Fife), and it may be suggested that these two sites, Cairnpapple and Balbirnie (which is only 350 yards from the henge at Balfarg), represent special centres of a sacred nature (fig. 18).

The first period of activity at Balbirnie is equivalent to the second at Cairnpapple, and consisted of a circle of standing stones surrounding a rectangular ritual enclosure built of low stone blocks set into the original land surface (fig. 19). Beaker pottery lay on this

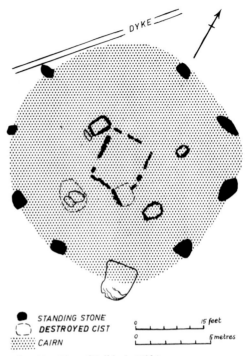

STANDING STONE
DESTROYED CIST
CAIRN

0 _____ 15 feet
0 _____ 5 metres

Fig. 18   Plan of Balbirnie (Fife)

surface. A series of stone cists set into pits were constructed after the abandonment of the ritual enclosure, and these correspond with the two cists of Period 3 at Cairnpapple. One of the Balbirnie cists contained a cremated burial together with a Food Vessel and a flint knife (fig. 15). A cup-marked stone had been re-used as packing material behind one of the side slabs of this cist. One of the slabs used in the construction of another cist was decorated with cup-and-ring carvings (fig. 20). Jet disc beads were found scattered over the site, and it is likely that these had originally belonged to one of the burials of this period, for there was some evidence that prehistoric grave-robbers had been at work on the site. Finally, a cairn of stones had been built over the entire area within the stone circle; patches of cremated bone and sherds of Cinerary Urns scattered amongst the stones of the cairn indicate that this final burial ceremony took place at approximately the same time as the enlargement of the cairn in Period 4 at Cairnpapple.

some religious or ritual significance. Good examples of cup-marks on standing stones may be seen at Easter Broomhouse (East Lothian) and Easter Pitcorthie (Fife). A flat

Fig. 19 Balbirnie, mortuary house (Fife)

CUP-AND-RING MARKS

One of the most puzzling features of the archaeology of the second millennium B.C. is the appearance in this area of the rock carvings known as cup-marks. These shallow circular depressions were pecked into rock surfaces, standing stones and sometimes the slab sides of burial cists. The cups, which measure about two inches in diameter and about half an inch deep, are occasionally surrounded by pecked rings or grooves as on the stone from Glencorse (Midlothian). Cup-and-ring marks have been the subject of much speculation; systems of writing, counting and even primitive calendars, as well as sun symbolism have been suggested as solutions, but it is unlikely that their real purpose or meaning will ever be known. Their association with standing stones and cists makes it probable that they have

slab from the cairn at Drumelzier (Peeblesshire) had been ornamented with four shallow double-ringed figures and a single ring. One of the side-slabs of a Food Vessel cist at Parkburn (Midlothian) was decorated with concentric semi-circles. There are also extensive areas of decoration on rock outcrops as at Bonnington Mains (Midlothian) and Castleton (Stirlingshire).

Several of these enigmatic slabs are collected in the National Museum of Antiquities of Scotland, including that from Lamancha (Peeblesshire) (fig. 21) and several from Edinburgh itself (fig. 46). The association of such carvings with cists and standing stones suggests in general terms a date in the middle of the second millennium B.C. A most unusual series of carvings occur on an almost inaccessible rock ledge above the River Esk at Haw-

Fig. 20   Balbirnie, cist with decorated side-slab (Fife)

thornden (Midlothian). Here there are circles, spirals and S-motifs as well as several more angular figures; these figures are quite unlike the more normal markings and they may be of a different date. A second flowering of this type of art is probably indicated by a number of cup-marks from souterrains and forts of the first few centuries A.D.

BRONZE WORKING

The introduction of metallurgy appears to be linked with the arrival of the makers of Beaker pottery, and the development of this new technology can be traced throughout the second and early first millennia B.C. Tools and weapons became successively more efficient

Fig. 21 Ring-marked stone, Lamancha (Peeblesshire)

and numerous as time went on. The metal-working process was improved by the use first of stone and later of clay moulds for casting objects, and, after about 900 B.C., by the addition of a small percentage of lead to the bronze thus improving the quality of the alloy for casting. An expansion of the bronze industry at about this time is indicated by a number of hoards of objects as well as by a numerical increase in the surviving bronze objects.

TOOLS AND UTENSILS

Small tanged knives, awls and flat axes were the earliest metal tools. Some of the axes bear incised or raised-rib decoration, and examples of these have been found in south-east Scotland at Falkland (Fife) and Harlaw Muir (Peeblesshire), (fig. 22). Flat axes were then replaced by a type with raised flanges, designed for more efficient hafting on to wooden handles (fig. 23). Around 1400 B.C., the tanged knives were supplemented by small blades and razors such as those from Stobshiel (East Lothian), Shanwell (Kinross-shire), Law Park (Fife) and Magdalene Bridge, Edinburgh. The final technological improvement of the bronze axe was made around the end of the 8th century B.C., by designing a socket into which

Fig. 22 Flat axes, Harlaw Muir, Innerleithen (Peeblesshire)

the handle could be inserted. A number of socketed axes have been found on top of Traprain Law (East Lothian), associated with structural traces of a settlement on the hill-top prior to the construction of a later fort. Fragments of clay moulds indicated that metalworking may have been practised on the hill.

Vessels made of sheets of beaten bronze riveted together were in use by this time, the seventh century B.C. Fitments from a bronze bucket have been found as part of a hoard of objects deposited in Duddingston Loch, Edinburgh. The cauldron from Hatton Knowe (Peeblesshire; fig. 26) testifies to the superb craftsmanship involved in the manufacture of such vessels; they may have been used for

cooking, for their broad rounded shape and ring-handles are essentially suited to suspension over a fire.

Harness fittings and cart mountings formed part of a hoard dating to about the 6th century B.C. which was discovered in 1864 under a stone on Horsehope Craig (Peeblesshire). The small size of these fittings suggests that they belonged to a miniature wagon, perhaps used for a ritual purpose.

HOARDS

One of the remarkable features of such Late Bronze Age finds is the number of hoards or collections of bronzes that have been discovered by chance. These appear to have been

Fig. 23 Flanged axes, near Peebles (Peeblesshire)

deliberately buried, in some cases as votive deposits but in others as part of the stock-in-trade or scrap pieces of itinerant merchants. Fourteen socketed axes (fig. 24) were found together on the edge of a cairn at Kalemouth (Roxburghshire), the central cist burial of which held a Food Vessel. Some of the axes have not been finished and it seems likely that this is a merchant's hoard dating to the late 8th century B.C. As many of the objects from Duddingston Loch are broken or bent and some are partly melted, it is safest to assume that these formed the raw material from which a bronze-smith intended to make new weapons; this is thus a founder's hoard.

Bronze armlets were evidently a fashionable type of personal ornament in Scotland from the 17th century B.C. onwards. Elaborate ex-

amples were found in the dagger-grave at Masterton (Fife), but plain forms also occur. Sheet bronze was beaten into covers for jet buttons early in the second millennium. In the Late Bronze Age some armlets were made of gold, and examples of these have been found in south-east Scotland at Kirk Hill (Berwickshire) and Alloa (Clackmannan). The gold is probably of Irish origin, though some may have been obtained from ores at Leadhills in Lanarkshire. By the mid-first millennium B.C., bronze was cast into pins of an elaborate form – known as swan's-neck sunflower pins – like that from Grosvenor Crescent, Edinburgh.

WEAPONS AND WARRIORS
Many of the bronze objects of the second and first millennia B.C. are weapons, either of an

offensive nature (like spearheads and swords) or of a defensive nature (like shields). The daggers often associated with late Beaker pottery were probably used for hunting and self-defence rather than in warfare, and the wooden bows and arrows tipped with flint belonging to this period were similarly used primarily for hunting.

Bronze socketed spearheads, halberds, dirks and rapiers were the principal weapons in the period from about 1400–900 B.C. and these may indicate more warlike conditions (fig. 25). The spearheads were probably attached to wooden poles and used for lunging rather than for throwing, since the metal was too valuable to risk losing. Dirks and rapiers would be used as stabbing weapons, and it is not until the stronger long-bladed sword was introduced in

the ninth century B.C. that the method of close combat changed from stabbing to slashing, although spearheads continued in use. Early examples of swords of the new type have been found in Crosbie Moss (Berwickshire), along with a spearhead, and in Poldar Moss (Stirlingshire). Slashing swords continued to be used till about the sixth century B.C. and are known from finds such as Auchencorth and Leadburn (Peeblesshire) and from the Arthur's Seat, Duddingston Loch and Grosvenor Crescent hoards in Edinburgh. The use of this type of sword implies some sort of shield, perhaps of wood or leather. The techniques of beaten metalwork discussed earlier made it possible to produce thin bronze shields dating to about the eighth century B.C. Three shields have been found at Yetholm (Roxburghshire), two in 1837

Fig. 24   Hoard of socketed axes, Kalemouth (Roxburghshire)

36

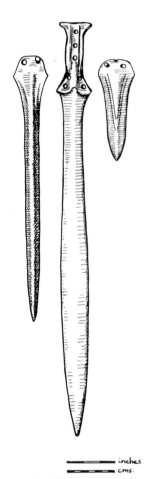

and one in 1870 near the place of the former discovery; on analogy with a find at Beith (Ayrshire), where five or six shields were found (regularly placed in a ring), the Yetholm shields were in all likelihood a votive deposit. They measure up to 24 inches in diameter and are decorated with concentric circles of small round bosses around a central boss which hides the handgrip. Experiments undertaken with a shield made exactly to the specifications of Late Bronze Age examples showed that they would have been quickly cut to pieces by the first blows of a slashing sword. These elaborately ornamented metal shields are thus ceremonial rather than for use on the battlefield. Leather shields dating from this period have been found in Ireland, and experiments showed that these would stand up well to similar attack and that they would have provided adequate protection. Although they were liable to go flabby in damp conditions this could be remedied, and the shield hardened, by immersion in hot beeswax or even boiling water.

TRAPRAIN LAW

Before about 700 B.C., possible centres of settlement can only be inferred from the distribution of burials and stray finds of pottery and bronzes, with the exception of Traprain Law. At this site, sufficient evidence of domestic occupation has been found to show that people were living on the hill-top before the later fort was built.

Traprain Law is an impressive isolated hill rising some 400 ft above the East Lothian plain. If we are right in suggesting that the Cinerary Urn burials found on Arthur's Seat and Braid Hills in Edinburgh represent hill-top settlements in the middle of the second millennium B.C. or rather later, it is interesting to find a similar situation on Traprain. Four Collared Urns and a small accessory vessel were uncovered in 1920 although only one still

inches
cms.

Fig. 25 Rapier (Midlothian); Sword, nr. Carron (Stirlingshire); Dagger, Kilrie (Fife)

37

Fig. 26 Cauldron, Hatton Knowe (Peeblesshire) and detail of ring handle

contained the remains of the cremation deposit. Evidence of occupation dating to about the seventh and sixth centuries B.C. is provided by a series of bronze objects including socketed axes, a spearhead and a number of tools. Fragments of clay moulds show that bronze working was being undertaken on the site and that spearheads, swords and socketed axes were being locally produced. Two socketed axes were found together close to the doorway of a small hut and a third axe was picked up not far away. The remains are difficult to interpret but seem to have consisted of an area of paving, a small hearth bordered by small stones and possibly a saddle quern and a cache of barley grains. The mass of stones round the hut may represent the tumbled and disturbed foundations for a wooden superstructure.

4 600 B.C.-A.D. 400: Fort-Builders and Iron-Workers

Settlement archaeology, or the study of purely domestic rather than ritual or funerary remains, begins in south-east Scotland after about 700 B.C. Despite the large number of bronze tools, weapons and ornaments of the early centuries of the first millennium B.C., none has been found on inhabited sites except those at Traprain Law. To some extent, this lack of association with settlements may be explained in terms of the value of metal, for such objects would be handed on through generations of families or melted down for re-use rather than thrown away or lost. This means that some of the known settlements

Fig. 27a   Palisaded homestead, Greenbrough (Roxburghshire), entrance

may have been contemporary with the manufacture and use of bronze artefacts, but cannot be so dated at present simply because their inhabitants took good care not to lose their most valuable possessions. An additional factor is involved, however, for the absence of known settlements datable to before the seventh century clearly cannot imply that no settlements existed, but simply that they did not exist in a form that would leave visible surface traces to aid later discovery. The earliest types of settlement known at present in south-east Scotland are those where clusters of houses were built on platforms cut into hill-side slopes (known to archaeologists as unenclosed platform settlements) or where houses were surrounded by a substantial timber fence (palisaded settlements). Traces of these sites survive in the form of visible depressions in the hill-side or visible grooves in the turf caused by soil subsidence into the bedding-trenches which originally held the upright posts of timber fences.

Earlier settlements must therefore have lacked any form of substantial enclosure. Some of the unenclosed platform settlements may belong to an earlier period than supposed at present, for there has been little excavation of this type of site and dating evidence is scarce, while similar clusters of timber houses, built not on hill-sides but on level ground, would escape detection altogether.

UNENCLOSED PLATFORM SETTLEMENTS

Examples of this type of settlement have been found in Peeblesshire, Lanarkshire, Midlothian and Roxburghshire. The number of house-platforms forming a settlement varies from two to twelve, and represents a social unit of one to perhaps four or five families. It must be remembered, however, that all the houses in a group may not have been in use simultaneously, nor need they all have functioned as dwelling-houses. Working-sheds and store-

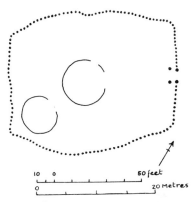

Fig. 27b Palisaded homestead, Greenbrough (Roxburghshire), plan

houses may also have been built. The platforms were constructed by scooping out earth and stones from the hill-side and piling this material in front of the scoop in order to level an oval or circular area. The average diameter of these platforms is 40–50 ft, but, in the case of the sole excavated example at Green Knowe (Peeblesshire), the timber structure which had been built on the platform occupied only the central area (a circle of about 30 ft diameter in a total available area measuring 50 ft across).

The platforms are sometimes grouped together in a cluster, but frequently they form a line along the contour of the slope, in which case it is possible that they represent the linear progression of a small homestead, where new successive houses are built on new sites a short distance from the abandoned houses. Two lines of platforms can be seen on the flanks of the White Meldon (Peeblesshire). Such a development may perhaps be seen also in the nucleated settlement on Glenwhappen Rig (Peeblesshire), where there is one group of seven small platforms and another group, some 200 ft away, of four large platforms.

The house excavated at Green Knowe proved to be of relatively unusual construction. The outer wall had consisted of a rough stone and earth or turf core, faced on either side by a wooden screen of withies woven between slender upright posts. The rafters had been supported by a ring of posts within the house, and the entrance had a cobbled floor. The upper part of a coarsely-made, barrel-shaped pot was found; this is not very helpful for dating the house, but a period around the middle of the first millennium B.C. has been suggested.

PALISADED SETTLEMENTS

A notable feature of south-east Scotland in the first millennium B.C. is the construction of homesteads and small hamlets surrounded by timber fences or palisades. Few sites have been excavated, but surface traces are often clearly visible in the short turf of the Cheviot hills, and many palisades have been recorded by field-work and air-photography on the ridges and spurs running west and south from the great Cheviot massif. Most of these sites lie in Roxburghshire and Peeblesshire, but outliers are known in Midlothian, Perthshire and Angus and it is likely that more are still to be discovered in such areas of south-east Scotland where surface traces do not survive as clearly as in Roxburghshire and Peeblesshire.

Before excavation, these sites are visible on the ground as areas of up to $2\frac{1}{4}$ acres delimited in most cases either by a single or by a double groove in the turf. There are sometimes traces of circular houses in the form of shallow depressions or rings in the turf. Most sites are approximately circular or oval, this being the most convenient form for building on hill-tops and spurs of land, but a few are sub-rectangular, like the small homestead on Greenbrough Hill (Roxburghshire; fig. 27).

Some of these settlements have been excavated, although, unfortunately, in every case only part of the area was opened up. The surrounding palisades or fences consisted of stout wooden posts set close together in a continuous narrow trench. These posts would presumably have been made stable above ground by horizontal wooden beams in much the same way as modern fences. Some sites, like Blackbrough Hill (Roxburghshire), were enclosed by a single line of palisade, while others, such as Gray Coat (Roxburghshire), had a double palisade set between 5 and 10 ft apart. Sometimes there was an outer palisade set at some distance from the main inner line of enclosure, thus providing, perhaps, space for penning animals. At Braidwood (Midlothian), for example, there was a gap of 46 ft between the inner and outer palisades.

Construction of these stockades must have involved considerable labour in cutting down and trimming a very large amount of timber, and good local supplies of timber must have been available. Most of the wood used at Hayhope Knowe (Roxburghshire; fig. 28) was alder, and it has been estimated that about nine acres of light woodland would have been cleared in order to obtain the required amount of timber. No axes have yet been found on any of these sites, but, if bronze or iron tools were used, the metal would probably have been melted down for re-use once the axes were broken or too worn.

The entrances into these settlements seem to have been closed by timber gates, and inside there were circular timber-framed houses. Some sites were evidently family homesteads with only one or two houses, while others were the homes of several families with a dozen or so houses. A single palisade on Glenachan Rig (Peeblesshire) enclosed an oval area, 108 by 84 ft, within which were two circular houses. Traffic through the entrance into the homestead had worn a hollow into the bedrock, and one of the houses and part of the surrounding palisade had been rebuilt during the lifetime of the site. The houses were of a simple form, consisting of a ring of posts forming the uprights of the wall frame and a central post to support the conical roof; rainwater dripping from the eaves had worn a shallow channel in the ground all round the house. An 8 ft long firepit in one house had held the hearth and still contained much wood-ash. The site lies on a slope above a burn which provided a convenient supply of water. There were no finds to date the period of occupation.

HAYHOPE KNOWE

Probably the best-known of the larger palisaded settlements is that at Hayhope Knowe (Roxburghshire), which lies on a spur of land projecting from the main ridge at a height of 1100 ft above sea level, overlooking a burn (fig. 28). Excavation has provided some detail of the features of this settlement, although only three of the twelve houses visible on the surface have been excavated. A double palisade enclosed an oval area, 300 by 175 ft, in which the houses appear to cluster in two groups leaving a free area in the centre of the settlement. There were two opposing entrances at either end of the oval, and the houses were built on either side of a 'street' between the two gates. An outer palisade encircled the site at a distance of some 17 ft.

Packing stones which had supported the upright posts of the main double fence were found in their original positions in the bedding trenches, showing that the posts had been about 8 inches thick and had been set about 1 ft apart. The twin trenches were linked together at the entrances, where post-holes indicated the use of timber gates; the east gate had worn a slight groove in the surface across the entrance. The three excavated houses were between 30 and 38 ft in diameter, each surviving in the form of two concentric grooves into which the frame of the outer wall and inner roof-supports had been set. Traces of a clay floor were found in one of them, and the hearth had been sunk into the floor. Fragments of coarse pottery, a clay spindle-whorl and an

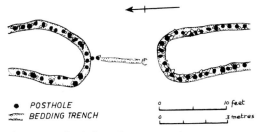

● POSTHOLE	
〰 BEDDING TRENCH	

0 ————————— 10 feet
0 ————————— 3 metres

Fig. 28   Palisaded settlement, Hayhope Knowe (Roxburghshire), detail of entrance

iron spearhead were recovered. Subsequently, an attempt was made to strengthen the settlement by means of a ditch and bank, but this was never finished.

Earthwork defences added to the palisaded settlement at Braidwood (Midlothian) were also left unfinished, but the reason remains obscure. Several sites were replaced by forts with ramparts of earth or stone, but we do not know exactly when this happened. In the cases where a palisade was replaced by a stone-walled fort, the change may have occurred as early as the sixth century B.C. Since artefacts are scarce among palisaded settlements in south-east Scotland, dating is obtained mainly by analogy with similar sites elsewhere. Bronze types associated with such a site at Staple Howe in Yorkshire and radiocarbon dates obtained from Craigmarloch in Renfrewshire and Huckhoe in Northumberland indicate that this type of site was well-established in the sixth century B.C. It is not known how long they continued to be built or occupied. The idea of enclosing a settlement in this way arose probably from the need to protect livestock from wild animals and raiders.

HAREHOPE

Occasionally, timber stockades were set on top of earthen banks instead of straight into the ground; this method seems to have been used in the last few centuries B.C. Excavation of one of these sites at Harehope (Peeblesshire) re-

43

Fig. 29 Distribution Map of forts in SE Scotland

vealed two major phases of construction, each of identical type and presumably not separated by any great length of time. Initially, an area of about 240 by 200 ft had been enclosed by twin banks linked together at the entrance and crowned by sturdy timber fences. Subsequently, a decision was made to strengthen the defences by building another pair of palisaded banks immediately within the original banks, thereby reducing the internal area of the site to 155 by 120 ft and doubling the protection. A timber-framed guardhouse was uncovered at the entrance. Excavation in the interior was confined to the central area, where three successive houses were found. The first two were of simple design, 24 ft and 20 ft in diameter respectively, but the third and latest house was both larger and more sophisticated in construction. It measured 36 ft in diameter, its outer wall had been set into a narrow bedding trench and the roof had been supported inside the house by a ring of posts each about 6 inches thick.

FORTS

Fortified settlements survive in south-east Scotland in greater numbers than any other class of monument dating to the period be-

44

tween about 600 B.C. and A.D. 100 (fig. 29). They have survived by reason of the scale of their defences and of their hill-top situations. Most hill-forts in this area are smaller than those in other parts of Britain, and it is sometimes difficult to distinguish a fort from an enclosed settlement. The distinction lies in defensibility; the enclosing walls and ramparts of hill-forts are larger and stronger than those of settlements.

The largest forts lie on Traprain Law (East Lothian) and Eildon Hill North (Roxburghshire), both enclosing about 40 acres and representing expansions of earlier smaller forts. These large forts are normally regarded as late tribal centres or *oppida*. Traces of 296 houses have been recognised within the fort of Eildon Hill North, suggesting a population as large as two thousand. This represents a density of some 50 people per acre, and, even with these approximate figures, it is clear that such a community cannot have been self-supporting and must have relied heavily on trade and exchange – a walled town in fact, comparable with small medieval towns. A large population inhabited the fort on Hownam Law (Roxburghshire), where at least 155 house-platforms are visible in an area of 22 acres. Such forts represent a highly organised and probably stratified society.

It is usually argued that the earlier and more numerous forts, enclosing a mere acre of land

Fig. 30   Fort, Woden Law (Roxburghshire)

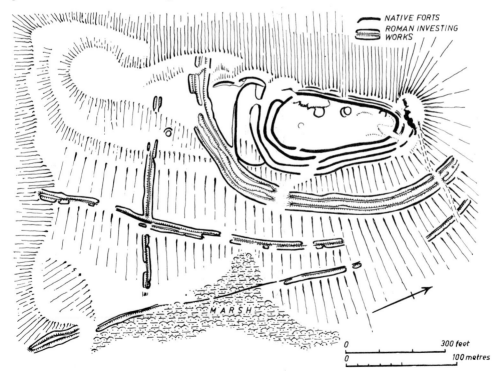

NATIVE FORTS
ROMAN INVESTING WORKS

MARSH

0 _____ 300 feet
0 _____ 100 metres

45

Fig. 31 Timber laced wall, Abernethy (Perthshire)

or less, represent a more fragmented society involving only very localised organisation. This may be so, but it is equally possible that overall tribal authority did exist but that it is not apparent in the archaeological record.

TIMBER-LACED FORTS

Stone and earth were the primary·materials used in building the defences of hill-forts, but timber was frequently used to strengthen and stabilize a wall or rampart of either material; for example the front of a rampart might be faced by close-set posts to prevent the loose material from collapsing into the ditch. Timber-lacing was also employed, whereby wooden beams were incorporated into the core of the wall or rampart, and evidence for this

practice can be found even without excavation in the form of burnt or vitrified stone. If the timbers in a stone wall were set alight, whether accidentally or deliberately by enemy action, the high temperatures obtained were liable to fuse the stone core into massive dark vitrified lumps. Evidence of vitrification has been found at Tinnis Castle (Peeblesshire) in the innermost fort wall, but one of the clearest examples of a vitrified fort is at Finavon, near Forfar (Angus). It is likely that many unburnt stone-walled forts would prove on excavation to have been at least partially timber-laced; the entrance into Castle Law fort (Midlothian) was flanked by timber-laced walling, although the rest of the rampart proved to be of plain clay without timbering. Clearance of way of the wall at Abernethy (Perthshire) revealed empty slots between the stones where timber beams had rotted away (fig. 31).

In recent years, radiocarbon dates obtained from samples of carbonised wood have indicated that timber-laced forts, or some of them at least, were among the earliest forts built in Scotland, dating from as early as the seventh century B.C. There were obvious limitations to the usefulness of the timber-laced method of construction; the risk of fire was considerable, replacement of rotten timbers involved dismantling the rampart, and large quantities of wood were necessary.

STONE-WALLED FORTS

There is reason to believe that stone-walled forts without any form of timber-lacing are earlier, on the whole, than forts defended by earthen ramparts. This has been demonstrated by stratigraphy at sites where a stone wall was succeeded or additionally strengthened by one or more ramparts, and radiocarbon dating of a stone fort at Huckhoe (Northumberland) has indicated that such forts were being built at least in the sixth century B.C. In south-east Scotland, the major excavated site at which a sequence of fortifications has been obtained is Hownam Rings (Roxburghshire). This site revealed three major phases of construction in its enclosing works, the first of which was a timber palisade. This was succeeded by a 10 ft thick stone wall with a rubble core faced on either side by laid stone blocks. Subsequently the entrance into this stone-walled fort was blocked up, and three earthen ramparts were built outside the wall with a new entrance. The site continued to be occupied after it had ceased to function as a fort, for houses with stone foundation-courses were built within and on top of the abandoned defences in the late third century A.D. It is not clear, unfortunately, how long a period of time had elapsed between the abandonment of the fort and the subsequent occupation, nor is there any dating evidence for the initial palisaded phase. Nevertheless, the sequence of building activities provided by the site is invaluable, and can, to some extent, be supplemented by dating evidence from elsewhere. Occupation may have begun as early as the sixth or seventh centuries B.C., and it is not unlikely that the sequence of defences spans the second half of the first millennium B.C. The dating of different types of fort defences, as with various types of non-defensive settlement of the pre-Roman Iron Age, is still a difficult subject, and all generalisations about dating are liable to be unsafe. Unfortunately, those sites that have been excavated have yielded frustratingly few artefacts, which are moreover of little help in dating; the pottery, in particular, is useless for dating purposes, for it is coarse and shows virtually no stylistic change. The more unusual artefacts which might be dated approximately by comparison with similar objects from sites outside south-east Scotland are naturally even scarcer than everyday objects like pottery and quern-stones.

EARTHEN FORTS

Without excavation, it is often difficult to distinguish between a collapsed stone wall and an earthen or rubble rampart. Since the choice of rampart or wall must have been governed to some extent by available building-material, the distinction need not be significant. Stone forts occur with a single wall (e.g. Woden Law, Roxburghshire) and with two walls (e.g. Dreva, Peeblesshire); and, similarly, earthen forts may have either one or two ramparts and ditches. Blackbrough Hill (Roxburghshire) is a good example of a fort enclosed by a single bank and ditch, and double ramparts with a medial ditch surround Harehope Rings (Peeblesshire).

MULTIPLE DEFENCES

Many forts were given additional lines of defences at a relatively late period of their occupation, usually in the form of one or more ramparts and ditches (figs. 30 and 48). Three such lines were added outside the stone wall at Hownam Rings, while a pair of ramparts and ditches were built to strengthen the original single-rampart fort at Castle Law. A few forts, such as White Castle (East Lothian), appear to have been designed with multiple defences from the beginning.

A number of forts in south-east Scotland remained unfinished, thereby providing interesting evidence of the way in which the defences were laid out and built. The line of the projected rampart was laid out on the ground by digging a shallow marker-trench; gangs of workers were then set at points along the line to dig the ditch and pile up the material into a rampart. Eventually, the sections of completed rampart were linked to form a continuous whole – unless the work were interrupted, as at Whitehill or Cademuir Hill 1 (Peeblesshire).

Most forts were built in strategic positions on hills and ridges. A striking exception is the multiple-ramparted fort of The Chesters, Drem (East Lothian), which is situated on a very low slope overlooked by a higher ridge; defence was clearly not a primary consideration here, and it is likely that this imposing structure was designed to impress. Apart from the firing of timber-laced forts, which may have been accidental, there is little evidence to suggest that hill-forts were attacked or besieged. This need not imply that they were all built purely for prestige, but that their defences were successful as deterrents.

OUTLYING DEFENCES

Apart from increasing the number of ramparts, two methods were adopted by the builders of hill-forts to provide outlying protection. One method was to construct a short linear earthwork across the approaches to the fort; such earthworks, or cross-dykes, consist normally of a bank and ditch, with the bank set on the fort side of the ditch. The most interesting example is that guarding the access route along the ridge to Harehope Rings. This is a classic example in its lay-out, for it spans the ridge with either end terminating at the point at which the scarp falls steeply away. The central portion is complete and consists of a bank and ditch, but at either end the earthwork tails off into discontinuous pits. It would seem that construction began by digging a line of pits, each with its own upcast material, and these were subsequently joined up into a continuous line of ditch and bank.

A similar earthwork bars the approach to the fort on Langlaw Hill (Peeblesshire). Its line impinges upon that of the outer enclosure of the fort, implying that it belonged to an earlier phase of occupation than that in which the stock enclosure was added. This dyke is unusual in having a distinct gateway through it, on the east side of which the ditch and bank turn in slightly towards the fort.

Outlying barriers of this sort may have been designed partly against wheeled or mounted traffic, but they might also be useful as pastoral boundaries to contain livestock close to the

Fig. 32 Terret, Muircleugh (Berwickshire)

Fig. 33a Sword chape, Houndslow (Berwickshire)

forts. The second type of outlying barrier was almost certainly designed to deter chariots or horsemen. This is known as *chevaux de frise*, and consists of a large number of pointed stones set upright and close together outside forts. Progress across such an area is made very slow by the necessity of picking one's way amongst the stones. At the fort of Dreva, the *chevaux de frise* are spread over an area of about 100 by 70 ft, protecting access up the slope from the south-west. At Cademuir Hill 2, the stones are spread along the flank of a gully on the south-east side of the fort. Recent excavations at Kaimes Hill (Midlothian) have revealed another example of *chevaux de frise*, now destroyed by quarrying. This type of defence work is rare in Britain, and the idea may perhaps be compared to the stake-filled pits at the Roman fort at Rough Castle (Stirlingshire).

TRAPRAIN LAW

Surface traces, partial excavations and abundant finds indicate a prolonged, and quite probably continuous, period of occupation on Traprain Law (East Lothian) from before the middle of the first millennium B.C. until the middle of the following millennium. If the history of the site during these thousand or so years were known in detail, it would provide a framework for the period which might be even more useful than that provided for the second millennium B.C. by Cairnpapple.

The fortifications on Traprain Law represent several successive phases of building, during which the extent of the area enclosed varied between 10 and 40 acres. This structural sequence cannot be tied in detail to a chronological framework, for, although some 600 small finds have been obtained from excavation, only a small part of the interior has been explored. Most of the objects belong to the late first century A.D. and later, and little is

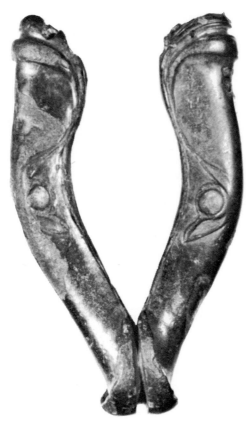

Fig. 33b   Sword chape, Glencotho (Peeblesshire)

known of the pre-Roman occupation. Metal-work datable to the late first and second centuries A.D. includes dress-fasteners, dragon-esque brooches, ring-headed and zoomorphic pins, glass bangles and bronze horse-harness fittings. Iron tools such as knives and sickles and weapons such as spearheads are not closely datable; it is probable that iron-working took place in the fort, and the evidence of clay moulds and crucibles demonstrates that bronze-working was certainly in progress.

There is thought to have been a gap in the occupation of the site in the late second and early third centuries, based on the evidence of coins and metalwork. Traprain was certainly flourishing again in the later third and fourth centuries, for the finds include both imported objects, such as Roman pottery, glass and coins, and locally manufactured goods such as brooches and pins.

In its final form, the fort was enclosed by a 12 ft-thick wall built of turf with stone facing, which surrounded an area of some 30 acres. The date of this final re-modelling of the defences is uncertain, but it has been suggested that it took place in the late fourth century.

HISTORICAL IMPLICATIONS

Classical sources, particularly the writings of Ptolemy, show that there were three major historical tribes in south-east Scotland at the time of the Roman invasion. Fife was inhabited by the *Venicones*, the area south of the Forth and down the east coast in the Lothians and Berwickshire was occupied by the *Votadini*, and the *Selgovae* lived around the Upper Tweed valley. The larger forts, and particularly the late examples with multiple defences, in these areas are normally attributed to the respective tribes on this geographical basis. In many cases, of course, this can be only a tentative attribution. Thus, forts such as How-nam Law, Yeavering Bell, North Berwick Law and Salisbury Crags are assigned to the *Votadini*, whose capital was surely the great fort on Traprain Law. The status of capital for the *Selgovae* is attributed to Eildon Hill North, with minor centres or *oppida* at the Dunion, Rubers Law and White Meldon. The fort at Norman's Law is postulated as the capital of the *Venicones*, none of whose other forts were as large as those of the tribes to the south. By the end of the first millenium B.C., a Celtic language seems to have become general in this area. The introduction of this language and of the more warlike way of life implied by defensive sites and Celtic weapons must indicate the arrival of a new, but possibly small, element in the population, but the precise context of this event is a matter of discussion amongst archaeologists.

SETTLEMENTS

The alternative to life in a hill-fort may be seen in the non-defensive settlements enclosed by earthen banks and ditches which appear to have succeeded the palisaded sites towards the end of the first .millennium B.C. One such settlement at Castle Hill, Horsburgh (Peeblesshire) contained at least three timber houses and was enclosed by double banks and ditches; this overlay an earlier and larger palisaded settlement. Similarly, at Kemp's Castle (Roxburghshire), a settlement enclosed by a single bank and ditch succeeded an earlier settlement almost twice its size. These, and other sites, support the suggestion that the social unit represented by non-defensive sites became smaller towards the end of the first millennium B.C. A small earthen-banked homestead, excavated at Scotstarvit (Fife), was found to have been occupied over a considerable period since three successive circular timber houses had stood within it. In several cases, the settlement was surrounded by a second line of bank and ditch, leaving a space between the two which was probably designed as an animal-pen.

These settlements contain circular timber-built homes and it is clear that, in general, settlements of circular stone-built houses are later in date than those of timber houses. Unenclosed groups of stone houses overlie the abandoned defences of hill-forts at Dreva (Peeblesshire), Hownam Rings (Roxburgh-shire) and other sites. The fort at Hownam Rings is also overlain by a stone-walled home-stead. Most stone-built houses seem to belong to the Roman period or later.

EARLY AGRICULTURE
Evidence for early agriculture is rarely found in south-east Scotland. A settlement of stone houses enclosed within a stone-faced wall was built inside the fort on Tamshiel Rig (Rox-burghshire), and it is unusual in being associated with a network of field walls covering an area of some 31 acres. Traces of cultivation within some of the enclosures have been recognised from air-photographs. The remains of another field-system have been found close to two stone-walled homesteads dating to the Roman period at Crock Cleuch (Roxburgh-shire). The field-system which lies along the north-west side of Dreva Hill and Dreva Craig was laid out after the fort had been abandoned. Although quern-stones have been found on a number of sites, including hill-forts, their presence is not reliable evidence for agriculture since grain can be traded in the same way as other commodities.

Three classes of monument found in south-east Scotland appear to represent intrusions by groups of people from outside the area, and their introduction to this area dates to about the second century A.D. (fig. 41). *Duns* are stone-walled structures, often occupying de-fensive positions. They have a solid wall, on average 10 to 12 ft in thickness, enclosing an

Fig. 34 Sword-scabbard, Mortonhall, Edinburgh

area about 40 ft in diameter. There is a distinct group in Stirlingshire with a number of outliers, but the main weight of their distribution shows that their builders came from Argyll and west Scotland. *Brochs* are circular, stone-built, forts with an internal diameter of between 30 and 40 ft; the wall, which might be over 40 ft high in exceptional cases, was built either with a spiral staircase or a number of cells within its thickness. Both systems of building enabled greater height to be achieved without adding unnecessarily to the weight of the wall. The majority of brochs occur in northern and north-western Scotland, and presumably the nine brochs in the south-east indicate invaders from these areas. The few *souterrains* or 'earth-houses' were probably the work of people from north of the Firth of Tay, because of their similarity to sites in this area. These monuments are long underground passages with dry-stone walls and they are roofed with lintel slabs, which are themselves hidden by earth and turf.

DUNS

The two well-excavated duns of Castle Hill Wood (Stirlingshire) and Stanhope (Peeblesshire) provide the best evidence of date for this group. The finds from the former include Roman glass and several quern-stones. The wall of Stanhope Dun encloses an area about the size of a small Iron Age house; a series of post-holes may suggest that the whole structure had been roofed over. The most important find for dating purposes was a small penannular brooch of a type dated to the late first and second centuries A.D. (fig. 38). There are a number of stone-walled forts which overlie earlier forts and which may be allied to a class of dun-like structures in Perthshire. It is difficult to find a satisfactory name for this group but the terms 'ring-fort' and 'citadel-fort' have been suggested. Size is perhaps the best distinction between duns, with a diameter of

some 40 ft, and 'ring-forts' which are often twice as large. Examples of this class of monuments are Dumyat (Stirlingshire) and Moncrieffe Hill (Perthshire). A small group, including Dalmahoy (Midlothian) and Dundurn (Perthshire), are likely to be of Dark Age date.

Fig. 35 Torc terminal and gold coins, Cairnmuir (Peeblesshire)

BROCHS

The only published modern excavation in this area is that of Torwoodlee (Selkirkshire); the site consists of a fort, in part at least defended by two earthen ramparts, and a broch additionally defended by an enclosing ditch. The fort was pre-Roman but the broch, which overlay it and whose ditch cut through the silted up ditch of the fort, contained pottery and glass of the late first century A.D. The basal part of the broch wall was solid with two cells or chambers built within it; it has been suggested that this method of construction, which can best be seen at Tappoch (Stirlingshire), is a late feature of the broch-building tradition. A series of post-holes were discovered within the broch. These probably indicate that an inner range of timber buildings had been constructed against the wall. The excavation showed that the broch had been deliberately and systematically destroyed to the lowest wall-courses not long after its building. The most likely explanation for this is that the broch was built by invaders from the north after the withdrawal of Roman forces and that, on the return of the Romans, the broch-builders lost or abandoned control of the area. The best preserved brochs south of the Forth are those of Edinshall (Berwickshire), Tappoch (Stirlingshire) and the Broch of Bow (Midlothian) in which an enamelled brooch in the shape of a cock has been discovered.

SOUTERRAINS

Typical of this class of antiquity is the souterrain at Castle Law which was built between the outer ramparts of the fort. The rock-cut ditch was widened and then lined with stone to form a gallery 72 ft in length. About halfway along the gallery, a narrow passage leads into a carefully-built chamber. Fragments of Roman pottery and glass as well as an enamelled brooch were discovered in the excavation and may suggest a date for its construction in the late second or third century A.D.

The souterrain at Crichton is about 50 ft long and has been roofed by flat slabs forming massive lintels with a 7ft span. The great interest of this souterrain is that about seventy of the stones used in its walls are of Roman origin. These are dressed and squared blocks, many of the outer faces of which have

diamond and diagonal chiselling, characteristic of prepared Roman stones. One lintel is carved with the figure of Pegasus, the Winged Horse. Roman stonework was also used in a souterrain near Newstead and in the walls of the 'citadel-fort' on Rubers Law, where it must have been plundered from a nearby signal-station.

The purpose of souterrains has long puzzled archaeologists, and no wholly satisfactory solution has been proposed. It seems unlikely that they were dwellings, at least of a permanent nature, because of their dank and cramped accommodation; for this reason the alternative name of 'earth-house' is out of fashion. They seem ill-suited as places of refuge as they would be difficult to defend and it would be easy to smoke out the inhabitants. The souterrain at Castle Law may have been built at a time when defence was of minor importance as it occupied the filled-up ditch of the fort. The suggestion that they are essentially underground barns either for storing goods or herding cattle has more to recommend it, although some would clearly be too damp to qualify for storing grain or meat over the winter, while others have too narrow an entrance to allow the cattle or sheep to enter.

Several examples of duns, brochs and souterrains have been found in secondary positions on sites already fortified or occupied. These include the brochs of Edinshall and Torwoodlee, the 'ring-fort' on the summit of Turin Hill (Angus) and the souterrain in the ditch of Castle Law. Evidence for their position and date, unsatisfactory though it is, comes both from their stratigraphical position and from the small finds recovered in the course of excavation.

WEAPONS AND WARRIORS

A very complete picture exists of the warrior of the last century B.C. and the first two centuries A.D., for not only have the weapons survived but Roman authors and sculptors have provided contemporary descriptions. The Romans may have stressed the disorganised nature of the Celtic armies. Dio Cassius gives a colourful description of the warrior barbarian of eastern Scotland in the third century A.D., and, although it is not an eye-witness description, it is a suitable introduction to an examination of warrior equipment. 'They go into battle in was a light two-wheeled vehicle drawn by two small horses which were harnessed by a yoke on either side of a central chariot-pole. The precise arrangement of the platform on which the warrior and the charioteer stood is uncertain, but a recent reconstruction (now in the National Museum of Antiquities of Scotland) favours semi-circular wicker side-pieces. The snaffle-bits of the horses were sometimes elab-

Fig. 36   Collar, Stichill (Roxburghshire)

chariots, and have small, swift horses; there are also foot-soldiers, very swift in running and very firm in standing their ground. For their arms they have a shield and a short spear, with a bronze knob attached to the end of the spear-shaft, so that when it is shaken it may clash and terrify the enemy; and they also have daggers.'

CHARIOTS

The war-chariot had gone out of fashion amongst the continental tribes by the second century B.C. and Caesar records his surprise at finding the Southern British tribes using them in the following century. In Scotland chariots were still in use in the early third century A.D. and, although no complete example survives, the decorative fittings still exist. The chariot

orately ornamented with enamel. Fixed to the yoke to guide the charioteer's reins were pairs of terrets, or 'fair-leads', and these might also be decorated; there are several examples from Traprain Law. Where groups survive, there are sometimes five terrets to a double set of harness with two pairs of leads for each horse and a single ring; the five terrets from Muircleugh, Lauder (Berwickshire) may form such a group (fig. 32). Two heavy terrets of 'Donside' type have been found in south-east Scotland at Eyemouth (Berwickshire) and Oxnam (Roxburghshire). These appear to derive from a terret in use in the Roman army and probably date to the late second century A.D.

SHIELDS

Very little is known about native shields in

55

Fig. 37   Stanhope hoard (Peeblesshire)

south-east Scotland; there are certainly no examples of the long oval shield of wood and leather current in England and perhaps the best evidence of the shield shape is on the Bridgeness distance slab. The Roman sculptor of this monumental slab showed four naked barbarians, one of whom has been speared in the back and another decapitated (fig. 40). Their weapons, which lie around in disarray, are a spear, a sword or dagger and two rectangular shields with round central bosses. These bosses were, we assume, normally of metal and were designed to protect the hand-grip of the shield; an iron fragment which may have been part of such a boss has been found in the votive deposit at Blackburn Mill (Berwickshire).

SPEARS AND SWORDS

The spears were long shafts, often of ash, with a leaf-shaped iron tip. Confirming Dio's description, there are examples of metal butts from Traprain Law. The sword of the Celtic warrior had an iron blade, was about two feet long, and had a hilt fitted round a tang. The scabbard was most frequently of wood or leather and was sometimes decorated with bronze fittings. Several examples of these have been found in south-east Scotland; two cast bronze chapes (fig. 33), objects designed to strengthen the tip of a leather sword-scabbard, dating to the first century B.C. come from Glencotho (Peeblesshire) and Houndslow (Berwickshire). A superb bronze sword-scabbard was found at Mortonhall, Edinburgh (fig. 34). Bronze alloys of two different colours have been used in the manufacture of this scabbard and there is an attractive contrast between the duller colour of the scabbard and the golden colour of the applied strip of open-work bronze on the suspension-loop. The Mortonhall scabbard belongs to a style of Celtic art current among the *Brigantes* in

north-eastern England in about the first century A.D.

Tacitus' description of the battle of Mons Graupius in A.D. 84 describes the more northerly *Caledones* and illustrates the way in which the superior weapons and organisation of the Roman army overcame the more flamboyant Celtic warriors: 'The battle began at long range; the Britons, with their long swords and short shields, showed both courage and skill in evading or brushing aside the Roman missiles, while on their side they launched dense volleys of spears.' Agricola then ordered his troops to fight at close quarters, a manoeuvre, 'embarrassing to the Britons whose shields were short and swords too long; for the British swords, without points, did not admit of locked lines and fighting at close quarters'. Agricola's troops routed the Caledonian foot soldiers as well as many of the chariots, some of which, driverless and with panic-stricken horses, darted across the battlefield.

PERSONAL ORNAMENTS

Celtic craftsmen lavished much skill on the production of elaborate decorated bronzework for the chieftain and his lady. Several personal ornaments have been found in the few burials of the period, including finger-rings from Granton and Gullane, and penannular brooches from Moredun and Craigie. By the second century A.D., Roman ideas of enamelling in several colours and almost mass-production may be seen in S-shaped 'dragonesque' and zoomorphic brooches.

NECK ORNAMENTS

In date the earliest examples of neck ornaments are those from the hoard discovered on Shaw Hill, Cairnmuir (Peeblesshire); three torcs all of gold, the golden terminal of a multi-strand torc and 'upwards of 40' gold 'bullet-shaped' coins were discovered. Of these only the terminal and two of the coins still survive (fig. 35). The coins belong to a type current in the Marne district of France in the first half of the first century B.C., and the torc terminal may be closely paralleled by the famous finds from Snettisham (Norfolk) of mid-first century B.C. date. The torcs were not made in Peeblesshire, but probably came from a workshop in eastern England, and may have been brought to southern Scotland either by a trader or by a refugee from the south.

The Stichill collar from Roxburghshire is an elaborate neck ornament of bronze, which is formed of two pieces hinged together, with a moveable join at the front (fig. 36). The decoration is a skilful arrangement of engraved spirals and scrolls side by side with hammered-up motifs. The collar is probably of second century A.D. date.

ARMLETS

A Roman *patera,* probably belonging to the mid-second century A.D., provides a date for the hoard from Stanhope (Peeblesshire), which contained an elaborate ribbed armlet and two decorated harness-fittings (fig. 37). The main areas of distribution, and probably manufacture, of this type are in Perthshire, Angus and Aberdeenshire and it has been suggested that their appearance may be connected with that of heavy bronze terrets and souterrains from these areas in the second century B.C. A rather simpler armlet of approximately the same date was found in a midden associated with the stone-walled fort on the summit of Wester Craiglockhart Hill in Edinburgh. In shape and decoration it is reminiscent of bracelets in the form of a coiled snake and the main concentration of this type is north of the Firth of Tay.

Many less important pieces were probably picked out with simpler decoration. There are no examples of carved woodwork which must

have been common, but there are a number of objects such as a bone comb from Ghegan Rock (fig. 38) and a decorated stone cup or lamp from Binney Craig (West Lothian) which are decorated in Celtic style.

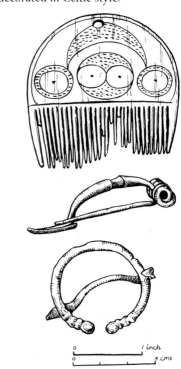

Fig. 38   Bone comb, Ghegan Rock (East Lothian); Bronze fibula, Abernethy (Perthshire); Bronze brooch, Stanhope dun (Peeblesshire)

VOTIVE DEPOSITS

Information about Celtic religion comes mainly from contemporary and later Irish literary sources, which are beyond the scope of this volume, but two archaeological aspects may be noted, namely ritual deposits in pools and the cult of the head. Deposits of metalwork from Eckford (Roxburghshire) and Blackburn Mill (Berwickshire) appear to be of a ritual nature. At the latter site sixty-three

Fig. 39 Moredun cist burial, Edinburgh

pieces of iron and bronze were discovered in two bronze cauldrons. Perhaps the greatest interest of these finds is the insight they provide into everyday life because of the range of ordinary tools found in them. Some of the pieces are of Roman origin, such as the second century *patera,* or of Roman inspiration, like the parts of a spring door-lock. The practice of venerating natural features and depositing objects in pools is known throughout the Celtic world. Many sanctuaries and shrines were associated with springs and rivers or were formed by sacred trees and groves and cannot, of course, be detected by any structural remains.

The cult of the human head as symbolic of divinity is also a common aspect of Celtic religion; stone heads probably decorated temple sites or shrines but are now almost exclusively found in isolation, as for example that from Muirton near Perth, and the sculpture found in Blackness Castle (West Lothian).

BURIALS

There are few burials of this period in Scotland but some of the most interesting are in the south-east. A cist, discovered at Moredun, Gilmerton, Edinburgh (fig. 39), contained two crouched inhumations with their heads at opposite ends of the cist. There were three iron objects in the cist – a projecting ring-headed pin and a penannular brooch at one end, and another brooch towards the middle. Perhaps the first two objects belonged to one burial and the brooch to the other; sticking to the underneath part of the brooch were the remains of a woven garment or wrapping in which the body had been buried. Another cist, found at Granton in the middle of the nineteenth century, also contained two crouched skeletons, a bronze spiral finger-ring and a penannular brooch. These are quite distinctive objects and provide a date for the cists in the later first or second century A.D.

A burial at Burnmouth (Berwickshire) was laid extended, rather than crouched, in a stone-lined grave and was accompanied not only by a short iron knife but also by two bronze objects, which have been interpreted as ritual 'spoons'. These enigmatic objects probably date to the first century A.D. The bones of a pig in the grave suggest that the deceased had been provided with joints of pork for his journey to the next world. This idea can be paralleled at a number of contemporary burials in Britain and on the Continent.

An irregular cairn of stones on the dunes at Black Rocks, Gullane (East Lothian), is probably of similar date. In the cairn material, and on the sand underneath it, were six inhumation burials, some of them certainly crouched. A bronze spiral finger-ring, an iron tanged knife-dagger and a sandstone whorl were the only objects discovered, but again they suggest a date early in the first millennium A.D.

Another form of communal burial was found at Lochend, Dunbar (East Lothian) where a massive cist was discovered. The structure was roofed by three capstones and was packed with the remains of at least twenty-one individuals. Parts of two iron penannular brooches and a bronze stud date the burial to the first or second centuries A.D. There is thus less uniformity in burial ritual than is apparent in the third or second millennia B.C. for example, and literary sources suggest that funerals were at this time more occasions for feasting than for communal religious effort such as cairn building.

Fig. 40 Detail of the Bridgeness Distance Slab (West Lothian)

5 The Roman Occupation

AGRICOLA

In A.D. 80, Roman armies under the general Gnaeus Julius Agricola marched across the Cheviots from Corbridge along the route that was to become Dere Street or later the A68, and also from Carlisle up Annandale and into the Clyde Valley. Agricola's purpose was to bring as much territory as possible under Roman sway. The advance cannot have come as a complete surprise to the native population, which must have known of the Roman presence in the south either through traders or possibly refugees like the owners of the Cairnmuir torcs. It is recorded, for example, that there was contact between the emperor Claudius and chieftains of the *Orcades*, usually taken to be the Orkney Islands. Some of the hillforts may have been strengthened in preparation for the attack; a number of forts, however, have secondary fortifications which appear to be unfinished, although this cannot be attributed with any certainty to Roman intervention. The Roman advance was initially into the territory of the *Selgovae*, possibly the Lowland tribe most hostile to them. Agricola's forces continued, seemingly unhindered by native resistance, through Lowland Scotland; perhaps the main reason for this lack of resistance was the absence of overall political organisation among the Celtic tribes.

The main axes of Roman operations in the south-east were dictated by their lines of communications (fig. 41); one followed Dere Street between Corbridge and the Forth, with a cross-route linking Newstead, on the Tweed, with the Clyde valley. The second line ran between the forts on the Forth, Inveresk and Cramond, and the Firth of Clyde through central Scotland. The third was between Camelon and the Perthshire forts of Ardoch, Bertha and Inchtuthil. As the Roman occupation of this area has already been described in a volume in this series, only an outline of the major sites will be given here. It should be remembered that the series of Roman occupations of south-east Scotland were prompted by military reasons and that no conscious attempt was made to bring the advantages of higher civilisation to the native population. Forts such as Newstead and Inveresk must have formed important focal points for local trade and administration. Native life probably went on much as before, although the use of hill-forts may have been forbidden and a number of undefended settlements of stone-built houses are found to overlie the remains of hill-forts.

In A.D. 80 and 81, Agricola established a temporary frontier on the isthmus between the Firths of Forth and Clyde, on the line that was later to be taken by the Antonine Wall. He consolidated his position with the construction of roads and forts in the south and even south-west of Scotland. Advance up Strathmore fired the Caledonians to make a stand at Mons Graupius, an unidentified site in the north-east, where they were decisively routed in A.D. 84. A second frontier was then established along the Highland line between Menteith (Perthshire) and Stracathro (Angus) with the legionary fortress at Inchtuthil (Perthshire) at the centre of the line. This

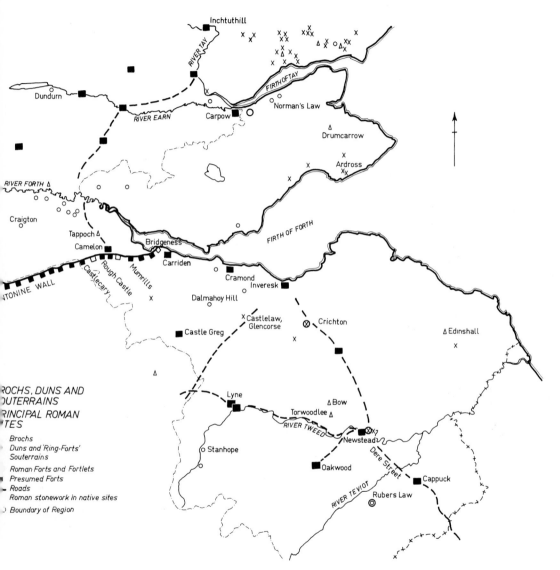

Inchtuthill

RIVER TAY

FIRTH OF TAY

Dundurn

RIVER EARN

Carpow

Norman's Law

Drumcarrow

Ardross

RIVER FORTH

Craigton

FIRTH OF FORTH

Tappoch

Camelon

Bridgeness

Carriden

Rough Castle

Murrills

Castlecary

Cramond

Inveresk

ANTONINE WALL

Dalmahoy Hill

Castlelaw,
Glencorse

Crichton

Edinshall

Castle Greg

ROCHS, DUNS AND
OUTERRAINS

RINCIPAL ROMAN
TES

Brochs
Duns and 'Ring-Forts'
Souterrains

Roman Forts and Fortlets
Presumed Forts
Roads
Roman stonework in native sites
Boundary of Region

Lyne

Bow

Torwoodlee

RIVER TWEED

Newstead

Dere Street

Stanhope

Oakwood

RIVER TEVIOT

Rubers Law

Cappuck

Fig. 41 Brochs, Duns, Souterrains and major Roman sites in SE Scotland

forward position was not held for long, and about A.D. 87, owing to a redisposition of legions, the frontier was abandoned and the forts systematically destroyed.

The key fortress for the new policy was Newstead, which was enlarged and strengthened, and which remained at the centre of Roman organisation in the south-east until the end of the first century A.D. when it was abandoned, possibly in the face of hostile action, and Roman forces were withdrawn from Scotland.

THE ANTONINE WALL

On orders from the Emperor Antoninus Pius, Roman armies advanced again into southern Scotland in about A.D. 140–1 under Lollius Urbicus, the governor of Britain. His orders were to establish a frontier between the Forth and Clyde, and the building of a permanent barrier was undertaken. The Antonine Wall was about 37 miles in length and ran between Bridgeness on the Forth and Old Kilpatrick on the Clyde. The wall was of turf construction on a stone base some 14 ft in width, and probably stood to a height of about 10 ft, with sloping sides and a summit width of about 6 ft. There was probably a wooden superstructure on the top of the wall, providing an outer palisade for protection, and a wooden duck-board-walk to stop erosion of the outer edges of the top and to provide a less slippery surface for patrols. To the north of the wall, and normally about 20 ft from it, was a ditch, approximately 40 ft wide and about 12 ft deep. To the south of the wall, and parallel to it, ran the military road, linking the forts in which the troops were stationed. Communication along the wall was no doubt mainly by messengers passing along the military road. Six signal posts have been discovered at various points on the wall, including two on either side of the fort at Rough Castle. These consist of square stone foundations built against the rear of the wall, which probably represent the bases of turf platforms on which beacon-fires were set. The beacons were probably used to send messages to forts in front of the wall rather than along it, for the system of beacons does not appear to have been continuous along the wall. The Wall forts were destroyed before A.D. 158, either by the northern tribes or by the Roman soldiers themselves in advance of withdrawal, and Newstead was again destroyed. Within a few years, the situation was restored and the wall again manned. The date for the end of the use of this frontier barrier is still a matter of discussion; currently there are two schools of thought which suggest either A.D. 163–6, or 197 or 207 for this event.

THE SEVERAN CAMPAIGN

About A.D. 200, the tribes of north-east Scotland attacked Roman positions further south; it has been suggested that the massive native armlets (fig. 37) and 'Donside' terrets found in the south-east date to about the time of these incursions. A punitive expedition was thought necessary by the Roman command to restore the situation. First northern England was consolidated, and then in A.D. 209–10, under the direction of the Emperor Severus himself, the *Caledones* and the *Maeatae* were defeated. The conditions of surrender were so harsh that the tribes rose again in A.D. 210–11, but they were spared a further campaign because of Severus' death in 211; his son, Caracalla, came to terms with the two tribes. Much of the supplying of troops for Severus' expeditions was probably undertaken by sea from a base at South Shields, with important coastal forts at Cramond, in Edinburgh, and at Carpow (Perthshire).

No troops were based in south-east Scotland under Caracalla; the frontier garrisons were positioned along Hadrian's Wall, and a system of patrols in the Cheviots gave advance warning of tribal movements. This brought

Fig. 42 Roman Fort, Lyne (Peeblesshire)

peace to the Lowlands for the next eighty-five years, after which the frontier was again attacked from the north by a people now known as the Picts – the descendants in all but name of the *Caledones* and the *Maeatae*. The northern tribes attacked Roman positions again in A.D. 364 and 367. The Roman sway over south-east Scotland was waning, and the *Votadini,* with their *oppidum* at Traprain, were entrusted with the protection of the eastern Lowlands. The treasure of silver objects found on Traprain, dating to the early 5th century A.D., seems to be a pirates' haul from a raid on the Continent and may show the continuing importance of this site (fig. 43). Din Eidyn (Edinburgh) became another centre of Votadinian power some time before the seventh century A.D., by which time they had become known as the historical kingdom of the Gododdin. Only in about A.D. 638 did the *Votadini* finally lose control over the Lothians and the lower Tweed Valley, when the advancing Angles captured their capital at Edinburgh.

Fig. 43   Vase   from   the   Traprain   Treasure
(East Lothian)

6 Edinburgh

The prehistoric sites and the chance small finds of bronze objects and cists from within the present boundary of the City of Edinburgh are a microcosm of the prehistoric period as a whole in south-east Scotland. Most of the small finds mentioned in this section are in the National Museum of Antiquities of Scotland, Edinburgh. The numbers in brackets refer to fig. 44.

Conventionally the story of Edinburgh begins with a discussion of the derivation of the name of the city and of the important defensive position of the castle. Although the Castle Rock is clearly one reason for the location of the city, it is possible to show, even in prehistoric times, a gradual increase in population in the area, with concentrations on hills such as Arthur's Seat. In the third and second millennia B.C., we may imagine the contours of the later city lightly forested with oak, alder and scrub, in parts badly drained and studded with lochs, and with those hills which still form landmarks rising above the tree cover. The massifs of Arthur's Seat, Braid Hills, Blackford and Wester Craiglockhart were clearly centres of population in prehistoric times. There is very little evidence of occupation by hunting communities, apart from a few flints from Arthur's Seat and from the Meadows, or of occupation by the earliest agriculturalists. There are, however, a few polished stone axes from the city, which indicate limited Neolithic activity in the area.

BEAKER AND FOOD VESSEL BURIALS

Two Beaker burials have been discovered but very little is known about them; one is from Craigentinny and the other was found in a cist at Juniper Green accompanying the burial of an elderly man. Both vessels belong to the later Northern groups. There are eleven Food Vessels, suggesting that, by the middle of the second millennium B.C., the population of the area had increased; three were found on the coast between Cramond and Leith, and four in the western suburbs at Juniper Green and Corstorphine. In 1884, a short cist was discovered at Merrilees Close, Yardheads, Leith, which held the remains of two crouched female skeletons and a Food Vessel placed near the larger of the two skulls. A cist containing a Food Vessel and a V-perforated jet button was found in Oxgangs Road, and each of two adjoining cists in Succoth Place yielded a Food Vessel. Several short cists containing the remains of a crouched inhumation have been found, but in each case there were no datable grave-goods; the sites of these cists include Barnton Golf Course, Bellevue Crescent, Craiglockhart House and Portobello Railway Station. During the construction of the Edinburgh to Granton Railway, a cist was discovered containing an inhumation and a necklace of cockle shells. There is a concentration of cists and also bronze finds along the line of the Water of Leith, from Leith to Juniper Green and along the coast of the Forth. Implements of the Early Bronze Age are very scarce; there are, for example, only two flat axes, one from Ravelston Hill and the other from Bible Land, Canongate. A twisted gold torc of Middle Bronze Age date, found during railway construction at Slateford, was lost when it was sold to a jeweller who melted it down (fig. 17).

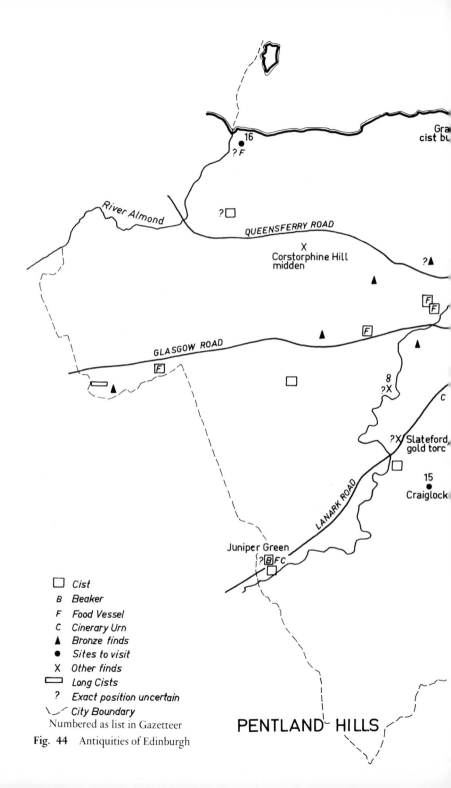

16
? F

River Almond

? □

QUEENSFERRY ROAD

X
Corstorphine Hill
midden

? ▲

▲

Gra
cist bu

F
F

F

▲

GLASGOW ROAD

▲

F

□

8
?X

c

? ▲ Slateford
gold torc

□

15
Craiglock

▲

LANARK ROAD

Juniper Green
? B F C
□

□	Cist
B	Beaker
F	Food Vessel
C	Cinerary Urn
▲	Bronze finds
●	Sites to visit
X	Other finds
▭	Long Cists
?	Exact position uncertain
⌣	City Boundary

Numbered as list in Gazetteer

PENTLAND HILLS

Fig. 44 Antiquities of Edinburgh

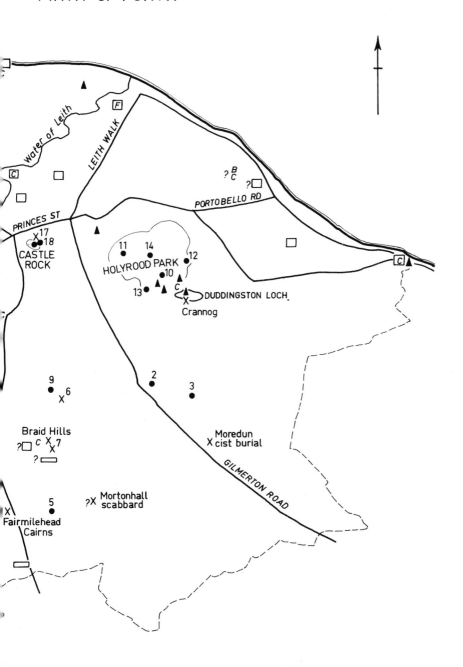

FIRTH OF FORTH

Water of Leith

LEITH WALK

F

C

PORTOBELLO RD

B
?C

?

PRINCES ST

X17
●18
CASTLE
ROCK

11 14
● ●
HOLYROOD PARK
● 12
10
●
13● ▲▲ C
X ▲ DUDDINGSTON LOCH
Crannog

C ▲

9
●
X6

2
●

3
●

Braid Hills
?□ C X X7
? ▭

Moredun
X cist burial

GILMERTON ROAD

5
●

?X Mortonhall
scabbard

X
Fairmilehead
Cairns

CINERARY URN BURIALS

At least sixteen Cinerary Urn burials, nine forming a cemetery at Magdalene Bridge, Joppa, may suggest an increasing number of people in the area and the idea of a cemetery, found here and at Kirkpark, Musselburgh, may indicate more settled farming communities. 'Urns', some of them now lost, were found during the building of the New Town, including several from Saxe-Coburg Place and during the digging of the North pier of the Dean Bridge. It is tempting to suppose that the urns and cists found on the Braid Hills and on Arthur's Seat indicate settlement on these hills about the middle of the second millennium B.C. or rather later. The discovery of cup-and-ring markings on Blackford Hill (6) and Braid Hills (7; fig. 46) provide further evidence of occupation about this time; another cup-marked stone from Edinburgh was found near Saughtonhall (8). There are one or two objects which belong to the Middle Bronze Age, including flanged axes from Corstorphine and Robertson Avenue, a dirk from Duddingston Loch and a small razor associated with one of the Cinerary Urns from Magdalene Bridge and the torc already mentioned from Slateford.

STANDING STONES AND CAIRNS

There are several standing stones in the southern part of the city, the most impressive being the Caiystane (fig. 45) near Oxgangs Road (1). This still stands to a height of over 9 ft and six cup-marks can still be seen on the back of the stone; there is also a large number of small natural depressions. Other stones which are of prehistoric origin are the Cat Stane at Kingsinch School (2) and a stone at the end of Ravenswood Avenue (3). These stones are near the lines of major routes and may have been put up as markers at a comparatively early date. The Cat Stane is rather smaller than is normal for standing stones, but its position

suggests that it may be accepted as one; it is now attractively incorporated into the playground of the school. The northern edge of the Pentland Hills near Fairmilehead must have been one area of settlement in the mid second millennium, for several cists have been discovered, including that with a Food Vessel mentioned above, as well as the standing stone from Oxgangs Road. There are also the remains of what was once an impressive cairn on the summit of Caerketton Hill about 1½ miles to the south of this complex (4). Two 'very large conical cairns', which were situated not far from the Caiystane, are frequently mentioned in accounts of the antiquities of the city; they were destroyed in the late 18th century when the nearby road was built, and stone settings or cists, with urns containing cremations, were discovered. Fragments of weapons including two iron spearheads were also found. There is another cairn a little to the east on Gallachlaw (5).

LATE BRONZE AGE FINDS

One phase of occupation near Arthur's Seat may be dated to the late 8th century B.C. by three hoards of bronze objects found in 1778 and 1846. A large collection of bronzework dredged from the bottom of Duddingston Loch contained many swords and spearheads in a broken or bent condition, some of them partly melted. We may, perhaps, imagine a primitive bronze foundry on the southern slopes of Arthur's Seat at this time, with the broken implements of this hoard forming the founders' raw material for future work. Some of the finished articles can be seen in two hoards discovered in 1846; one consists of two socketed axes and the other of two bronze leaf-shaped swords. A bronze sword and chape were found at Gogarburn House near Corstorphine. Rather later in date (about 550 B.C.) is the hoard of about fourteen bronze swords with a ring and a swan's-necked sunflower-

Fig. 45   Caiystane, Edinburgh

Fig. 46 Cup-marked-stone, Braid Hills, Edinburgh

headed pin from Grosvenor Crescent. The distribution of Late Bronze Age objects, along with those of earlier periods, may confirm the general suggestion of a steadily increasing population in the area, and from the evidence of the small finds alone, we may perhaps suggest centres on Arthur's Seat, in Corstorphine, Juniper Green and Leith.

THE IRON AGE

The most important Iron Age finds from the city have already been mentioned; they are the bronze sword-scabbard from Mortonhall (fig. 34), and the cist burials from Moredun (fig. 39) and Granton. Settlement on the north-west end of Corstorphine Hill, probably of Iron Age date, is implied by the presence of midden deposits containing fragments of pottery, stone pounders, a whorl and a bone implement. The middens were found during quarrying operations in the 1890's. There is a small stone-built fort on Wester Craiglockhart Hill (15), where a twisted bronze armlet has been found; the fort occupies a prominent knoll, and traces of its drystone walling are still visible. Faint indications of fortification survive on Blackford Hill. It is probably safe to assume the former existence of a fort on the Castle Rock for, although all traces have been obliterated by later building, it is unlikely that so defensible a situation should have been ignored.

Fig. 47   Pictish Symbol Stone, Princes Street Gardens, Edinburgh

HOLYROOD PARK

The most impressive remains of prehistoric monuments are in Holyrood Park, and those most worth visiting are the fortifications or enclosures on Salisbury Crags (12), Arthur's Seat (10) and Dunsapie Hill (11), all broadly of Iron Age date. The nose of Salisbury Crags was defended by a stone wall about 650 yards long and enclosing an area of about 25 acres. The east slopes of Arthur's Seat were fortified by a pair of formerly impressive stone ramparts, 375 yards long, enclosing an area of 20 acres. This fort and that on Salisbury Crags are among the larger forts of south-east Scotland. Another fort, above Samson's Ribs, has recently been discovered on Arthur's Seat (13); a Roman finger-ring, found within the fort, has a sardonyx intaglio of Mediterranean origin set in the remains of an iron band. A further fortification occupies the small volcanic summit to the east of Dunsapie Loch; this has been defended by a stone wall but it is now rather difficult to trace. It is possible that there are the remains of hut platforms in the east half of the interior of the fort. A group of six small hut-circles occupies one of the Dasses (14), a series of platforms in the hill-side to the east of Hunter's Bog; the foundations of the huts, which are about 20 ft in diameter, are now very ruined, but they seem to form a compact linear village about 150 ft in length. The evidence for the crannog, or lake-side dwelling, in Duddingston Loch is unsatisfactory, although wooden piles have certainly been recorded about the centre of the southern side of the Loch.

CRAMOND FORT

The fort at Cramond (16) is the only Roman site within the city. Part of the site has been laid out to show the plan of the internal features, and a model, together with the finds from the excavations, is in the City Museum at Huntly House. The fort was built partly to serve the Antonine Wall forts in the middle of the second century A.D., and was reconstructed as a vital port during the Severan campaign. The interior of the fort covers a little more than 5 acres, an area larger than is usual for its size of garrison, and this was designed to accommodate granaries and storehouses. The headquarters building, workshops and a latrine were also discovered in the course of the excavations.

THE DARK AGES

There are few monuments or objects which can be dated to the immediately post-Roman period, but at about this time the area became the major seat of the rulers of the kingdom of the Gododdin (the descendants of the Votadini), and the name Din Eidyn came into use. This is probably derived from a Celtic word 'Eidyn', and the word for a stronghold, 'dun'. From Din Eidyn, the warriors of the Lothians marched to defeat at the battle of Catreath (probably Catterick in Yorkshire), which was commemorated in the poem 'The Gododdin'. With the advance of the Angles from Northumbria, the Lothians were lost little by little, and, after a siege in A.D. 638, Edinburgh fell to the invaders and a new phase of its history begins.

Dating to the middle of the first millennium we may note a Pictish symbol stone (fig. 47), found in Princes Street Gardens (17), although this may not have been its original position, and now preserved in the National Museum of Antiquities; this is one of the very few examples from south of the Forth and is decorated with a crescent and V-rod symbol and part of a circular symbol. The visitor should not be misled by the Runic stone of the Viking Age (18) set up in Princes Street Gardens beneath the Castle Esplanade; it is not a native monument but comes from Witting parish, Westmanland in Central Sweden and was presented to the Gardens by the Society of

Fig. 48 Fort, Whiteside Hill (Peeblesshire)

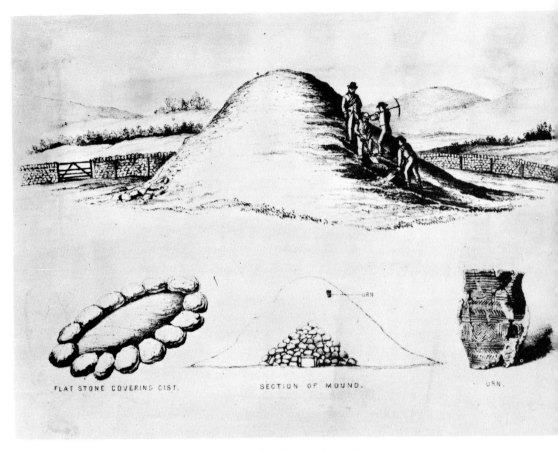

Fig. 49 Opening the Fairy Knowe, Pendrich (Stirlingshire) 1868

Antiquaries of Scotland. The inscription reads 'Ari put up this stone in memory of his father Hjálm. God help his soul'. Several long cists bear witness to a Christian population in Edinburgh in the middle of the first millennium A.D.; these have been found on the Lothianburn and Mortonhall golf courses in the southern part of the city, and at Gogarburn near the western boundary.

The siting of the Scottish capital was not of course affected by the antiquity of settlement in the area, but by the dual considerations of the defensibility of the Castle Rock, along with the ridge on which the town was built, and its position at the centre of East Coast communications by land and sea. Neither consideration would be of much importance to the Bronze Age population of cist builders, but, with the nucleus of finds in Holyrood Park, it is perhaps possible to see the area's growing importance as a regional centre as early as the Late Bronze Age and Early Iron Age.

Gazetteer of Sites

The following gazetteer includes representative examples of the various types of site discussed in this volume; many others are described in the detailed R.C.A.M.S *Inventories*. Some of the most impressive sites are hill-forts and these are listed in greater number than other monuments but with less descriptive detail. Many of the sites are on private ground and the intending visitor should always seek prior permission from the landowner and the farmer.

The following abbreviations are used:

D.E.S.:   *Discovery and Excavation, Scotland*

Feachem: R. Feachem, *A Guide to Prehistoric Scotland*, 1963

N.M.A.:   National Museum of Antiquities of Scotland, Edinburgh

P.S.A.S.:   *Proceedings of the Society of Antiquaries of Scotland*

R.C.A.M.S.:   Royal Commission on the Ancient and Historical Monuments of Scotland, followed by the county of *Inventory*

BERWICKSHIRE

ADDINSTON

Fort
NT 523536; Sheet 63. 1m E of Carfraemill.
Impressive fort with two ramparts.
R.C.A.M.S. *Berwickshire*, no. 213, p. 110–2; Feachem, 113.

BORROWSTOUN RIG

Stone Circle
NT 560521; Sheet 63. 3¼m ESE of Carfraemill; 1m NE of the summit of Dabshead Hill, where there are the remains of a fort, via the farm of Burncastle. At least 32 stones of this egg-shaped ring survive forming a circle approximately 150 ft by 140 ft. The stones are small and some barely project above the heather.
R.C.A.M.S. *Berwickshire*, no., 226, p. 120; A. Thom, *Megalithic Sites in Britain*, 1967, 69–70.

EARN'S HEUGH

Forts
NT 892691; Sheet 64. 2m NNW of Coldingham; road to Waterside farm, then walk. Two forts side by side on the edge of a sheer cliff.
R.C.A.M.S. *Berwickshire*, no. 80, p. 45–6; *P.S.A.S.*, lxvi (1931–2), 152–83; Feachem, 112.

EDINSHALL

Fort and Broch
NT 772603; Sheet 63. 2¼m NW of Preston (signposted; in the care of the Department of the Environment).
The earliest remains are those of a hill-fort, measuring overall 580 by 375 ft, with its entrance to the W; the secondary broch lies in the NW corner of the defences. It measures about 55 ft in diameter within a wall up to 17 ft in thickness. There are five

chambers within the thickness of the wall, including a guard-cell on either side of the entrance and a staircase giving access to the top of the wall. There are also a number of later buildings within the fort.
R.C.A.M.S. *Berwickshire*, no. 115, p. 60–4; Feachem, 111–2.

HABCHESTER
Fort
NT 944588; Sheet 64. 2m SE of Ayton; W end of Lamberton Moor; remains of fort with two ramparts.
R.C.A.M.S. *Berwickshire*, no. 270, p. 153–4; Feachem, 112–3.

THE MUTINY STONES
Long Cairn
NT 622590; Sheet 63. 4½m WNW of Longformacus.
This impressive cairn stands above the valley of the Dye Water in the moorland of the Lammermuir Hills. The cairn is aligned NE-SW, with its broader and higher end to the NE, and is about 280 ft in length and between 75 and 25 ft in width. Though robbed to provide material for sheep-stells nearby, it still stands to about 8 ft at the E end. The stretch of dry-stone walling found within the cairn, some 22 ft from its E end, during excavation in 1924 can no longer be seen.
R.C.A.M.S. *Berwickshire*, no. 249, p. 130–1; *P.S.A.S.*, lix (1924–5), 198–204; Feachem, 42.

EAST LOTHIAN

BLACK CASTLE
Fort
NT 580662; Sheet 63. 3m SE of Gifford.
Well-preserved fort with two ramparts.
R.C.A.M.S. *East Lothian*, no. 50, p. 34–5; Feachem, 123.

THE CHESTERS, DREM
Fort
NT 508783; Sheet 63. ¾m S of Drem (in the care of

the Department of the Environment).
An impressive fort with well-preserved ramparts; unusual because of its low-lying and overlooked position.
R.C.A.M.S. *East Lothian*, no. 13, p. 9–10; Feachem, 119–20.

EASTER BROOMHOUSE
Standing Stone
NT 681766; Sheet 63. In the middle of a field 200 yds S of Easter Broomhouse farm. Standing stone, 9 ft in height, with three cup-markings on the W face.
R.C.A.M.S. *East Lothian*, no. 174, p. 110.

FRIAR'S NOSE
Fort
NT 664632; Sheet 63. At the angle of the Whiteadder Water and the Killmade Burn, 8½m ESE of Gifford.
On the W side four ramparts survive of this well-preserved fort; entrance on NE.
R.C.A.M.S. *East Lothian*, no. 219, p. 136–7; Feachem, 123.

HARELAW
Fort
NT 546631; Sheet 63. 3¼m SSE of Gifford. on the summit of Harelaw.
The remains are those of a stone-walled fort, the timber-lacing of which has been set alight and caused patches of vitrifaction; the fort has measured some 200 ft by 100 ft. There are also traces of a number of outworks.
R.C.A.M.S. *East Lothian*, no. 254, p. 149–50; Feachem 122–3.

KIDLAW
Fort
NT 512642; Sheet 63. 300 yds E of Kidlaw; 2¾m SW of Gifford.
Fort with three ramparts, with entrances on the E and W.
R.C.A.M.S. *East Lothian* no. 259, p. 153–4; Feachem, 122.

KINGSIDE HILL, MAYSHIEL

Stone Circle
NT 627650: Sheet 63. 6½m SSE of Gifford on NW slope of Kingside Hill. This circle is about 39 ft in diameter and consists of 30 small boulders; there is a small central mound with a further stone in the centre of it.
R.C.A.M.S. *East Lothian*, no. 240, p. 141; Feachem, 76.

KIRKLANDHILL

Standing Stone
NT 616776; Sheet 63. 300 yds SW of Kirklandhill. Impressive stone stands at a road junction; 11 ft in height.
R.C.A.M.S. *East Lothian*, no. 206, p. 131–2, Feachem, 75.

TRAPRAIN LAW

Fort
NT 581746; Sheet 63. 4m E of Haddington.
Traprain Law is an isolated ridge which rises abruptly above the East Lothian plain to a height of 724 ft OD; the sequence of occupation or activity on the site makes it one of the most important in SE Scotland. The discovery of several Cinerary Urns might suggest that the hill-top was occupied in the mid-2nd millennium B.C.; certainly by the Late Bronze age there was structural evidence of settlement as well as a series of razors, socketed axes and other tools, together with a number of moulds showing that spears, swords and axes were made on the site. The most visible remains today are those of the rampart at the base of the hill on the N and taking in the flat platform on the W, enclosing an area of about 40 acres. This fort dates to the early centuries A.D. and, as the capital of the Votadini, must have been one of the most important centres in the area. The massive stone wall, which is rather higher up the hill on the N side and overlies the earlier wall on the W, encloses an area of about 30 acres. It has been suggested that this fort dates from about A.D. 370 when the Votadini were entrusted by the Romans with the protection of the Lothians.

In 1919 a hoard of Roman silver plate was discovered in a pit beneath an occupation level; more than 160 pieces were found, including flagons, goblets, bowls and dishes (fig. 43). Coins found with the silver suggest that it was deposited about the beginning of the 5th century A.D. Much of the silver had been ruthlessly cut up or squashed and folded into small packets – and this may indicate that it was pirate booty looted from the Continent.
Areas of rock surface with cup-and-ring markings, incised lines and symbols were discovered during quarrying in 1931; portions of the rock and casts of the decoration are in the N.M.A.
P.S.A.S., lxxxix (1955–6), 118–226; 284–9 (for refs.); Feachem, 120–1; A. O. Curle, *The Treasure of Traprain*, 1923; *P.S.A.S.*, lxix (1934–5), 122–37 (decorated rock surfaces).

YADLEE

Stone Circle
NT 654673; Sheet 63. 300 yds SE of Yadlee.
Circle of seven small stones just protruding above ground level; 27 ft in diameter.
R.C.A.M.S. *East Lothian*, no. 172, p. 110; Feachem, 76–7.

EDINBURGH (fig. 44); Sheet 62

Standing Stones and Cairns
1. Caiystane, Caiystane View, Oxgangs Road (NT 242683) (fig. 45)
   R.C.A.M.S. *Midlothian*, no. 19, p. 16; Feachem, 81.
2. Cat Stane, Inch (NT 274706)
   R.C.A.M.S. *Midlothian*, no. 163, p. 134.
3. Standing Stone, Ravenswood Avenue (NT 282705)
   R.C.A.M.S. *Midlothian*, no. 165, p. 134 (Greenend).
4. Cairn, Caerketton Hill (NT 237662)
   R.C.A.M.S. *Midlothian*, no. 145, p. 116; Feachem, 81.
5. Cairn, Gallachlaw (NT 254682).

Cup-Marked Stones

All are now in the National Museum of Antiquities of Scotland, Edinburgh; see *P.S.A.S.*, c. (1967–8), 70–1.

6. Blackford Hill (NT 256704), cup-and-ring markings, some with radial grooves.
R.C.A.M.S. *Midlothian*, no. 228, p. 167.

7. Braid Hills (NT 253696), three cup-and-ring markings, two with radial grooves and four cups (fig. 46).
R.C.A.M.S. *Midlothian*, no. 229, p. 167.

8. Saughtonhall (position not known), twelve cup-markings.

Forts and Hut Circles

9. Blackford Hill (NT 254706)
R.C.A.M.S. *Midlothian*, no. 227, p. 167.

10–14. Holyrood Park:

10. Arthur's Seat (NT 278729); 11, Dunsapie (NT 282731); 12. Salisbury Crags (NT 270732); 13. Samson's Ribs (NT 274725); 14. Hut Circles, The Dasses (NT 274732)
R.C.A.M.S. *Midlothian*, no. 10, p. 9–10; *City of Edinburgh*, nos. 208–10, p. 247–8; *P.S.A.S.*, lxxxi (1946–7), 158–70; *Burlington Magazine*, cxii (1970), 307, for intaglio. Other sites in Holyrood Park include the crannog in Duddingston Loch (*P.S.A.S.*, vi [1864–6], 161–2) and a number of Dark Age and Medieval monuments on the slopes of Arthur's Seat, including cultivation terraces, which have been fully described in *P.S.A.S.*, lxxxi (1946–7), 158–70.

15. Wester Craiglockhart Hill (NT 228700)
R.C.A.M.S. *Midlothian*, p. xxviii; *D.E.S. 1970*, 32.

16. Roman Fort, Cramond (NT 190768)
University of Edinburgh Journal, xx (1962), 305–8.

Dark Age

17. Pictish Symbol Stone, Princes Street Gardens (now in the National Museum of Antiquities of Scotland) found near the Well-House Tower below the Castle in use as a footbridge on a garden path (fig. 47).
J. R. Allen, *Early Christian Monuments of Scotland*, 1903, vol. iii, 421; R.C.A.M.S. *City of Edinburgh*, no. 159, IB 1, p. 215; *P.S.A.S.*, lxxxiv (1949–50), 207.

18. Rune Stone, Princes Street Gardens (NT 252735)
Archaeologia Scotica, ii (1822), 490–1, pl. xvi; *Sveriges Runenskrifter*, ix (1953–8), 653–6.

FIFE

BALBIRNIE

Stone Circle
NO 285030; Sheet 56.
The excavation of this site has been fully described in the text; the circle was excavated in advance of road-building operations and it has been reconstructed about 100 yds SE of the original site by Glenrothes Development Corporation.
D.E.S. 1970, 61–2.

BALFARG

Henge and Standing Stones
NO 281031; Sheet 56. 1½m NW of Markinch.
Only two standing stones survive to indicate the position of a henge which has been identified as a crop-mark on an air photograph. One stone is set just outside the entrance gap and the other may be interpreted as the only remaining example of a circle within the area enclosed by the ditch. The overall diameter of the site was about 300 ft.
P.S.A.S., lxxxiv (1949–50), 58–9; Feachem, 65.

DUNEARN HILL

Fort
NT 211872; Sheet 55. 1¼m NW of Burntisland.
Two periods are represented, the earlier by a single stone-walled fort, the second by a possible 'ring-fort' which measures 120 ft in diameter.
Feachem, 124–5.

EASTER PITCORTHIE

Standing Stone
NO 497640; Sheet 56. 600 yds NW of farmhouse; 2½m N of Elie.

A red sandstone block about 8 ft in height; on the S face of the stone there are thirty-three cup-marks and two 'dumb-bell' figures.
R.C.A.M.S. *Fife*, no. 88, p. 48.

GREENHILL

Cairn
NO 345228; Sheet 56. ½m W of Coultra farm; 4m SW of Wormit.
This cairn is about 50 ft in diameter and 5 ft in height; excavation showed that the cairn covered a number of cists; Food Vessels and a jet necklace were found.
P.S.A.S., xxxvi (1901–2), 635–53; Feachem, 78.

LUNDIN LINKS

Standing Stones
NO 404026; Sheet 56.
To the W of Lundin Links are three of the most impressive stones in this region, standing 13 ft 6 in, 17 ft and 18 ft in height; at least one other stone is known to have existed at the end of the 18th century.
R.C.A.M.S. *Fife*, no. 379, p. 186; Feachem, 77.

NORMAN'S LAW

Fort
NO 305203; Sheet 56 5½m NW of Cupar.
A multi-period fort with, at the highest point of the hill, a stone 'ring-fort' (measuring 100 by 170 ft within a wall up to 16 ft thick); this can be compared to similar structures on Turin Hill, Dunearn, Dumyat and Moncrieffe Hill.
R.C.A.M.S. *Fife*, no. 193, p. 104–5; Feachem, 125.

TORRY

Standing Stone
NT 028866; Sheet 55. 4m W of Dunfermline; beside an AA box.
The stone stands 8 ft high and is decorated on all faces with a number of cup-marks; there are also natural vertical grooves. There is a setting of three

boulders 60 ft to the SW of the standing stone.
R.C.A.M.S. *Fife*, no. 526, p. 273.

KINROSS-SHIRE

DRUMGLOW

Fort and Cairn
NT 076965; Sheet 55. 4½m SW of Kinross.
Four lines of defence cut off the only easy line of approach to a broad promontory in the massif of the Cleish Hills. Within the fort there is a cairn some 50 ft in diameter; when this was excavated in 1904 a tree-trunk coffin was discovered.
P.S.A.S., xxxix (1904–5), 179–81; R.C.A.M.S. *Kinross-shire*, nos. 549–50, p. 290.

MIDLOTHIAN

BOW

Broch
NT 461417; Sheet 62. 2m S of Stow.
The broch stands on a level shelf 450 ft above the left bank of the Gala Water; part of the wall is well-preserved and the outline of the rest is clearly visible.
R.C.A.M.S. *Midlothian*, no. 233, p. 169; Feachem, 166.

BRAIDWOOD

Settlement
NT 193596; Sheet 62. ¾m SW of Silverburn Village.
This well-preserved settlement lies on a spur of the Pentland Hills above the Eight Mile Burn. In its original form, an area of about 180 by 120 ft was enclosed by a timber palisade, the line of which is still visible on the ground, with an outer palisade at a distance of some 46 ft and a single entrance. This timber enclosure was subsequently replaced by two earthen banks constructed on the same line as the outer palisade and using the same entrance. The

sites of more than a dozen houses are visible on the ground as slight depressions.

R.C.A.M.S. *Midlothian*, no. 206, p. 156–7; *P.S.A.S.*, lxxxiii (1948–9), 1–11; xci (1957–8), 61–6 Feachem, 135–6.

CASTLE GREG

Roman Fortlet

NT 050592; Sheet 61. 3m SE of West Calder.

The fortlet survives almost intact; it measures about 150 by 180 ft with a single rampart and double ditches. The entrance is on the E.

R.C.A.M.S. *Midlothian*, no. 177, p. 140–1.

CASTLE LAW, GLENCORSE

Fort and Souterrain

NT 229638; Sheet 62. 3m S of Fairmilehead; under the protection of the Department of the Environment; key to souterrain from D.O.E., Argyle House, Edinburgh.

The visible remains are those of an eroded fort and a well-preserved souterrain. Excavation has shown that there was originally a palisaded enclosure, followed by a single-rampart fort with timber-lacing near its entrance, succeeded by a more elaborate fort.

The innermost fort ditch was subsequently expanded, and a souterrain was built in it; the entrance is to the N and the passage, 65 ft long and 3 to 6 ft 6 in wide, is over 5 ft high, with its sides constructed of dry-stone walling. Halfway along there is a short passage which leads to a cell, 11 ft 6 inches in diam.; its corbelled wall still stands to a height of over 6 ft. The finds, which include a brooch, Roman pottery and glass, belong to the 2nd century A.D.

P.S.A.S., lxvii (1932–3), 362–88; lxxxvi (1951–2), 191–4.

CRICHTON

Souterrain

NT 400619; Sheet 62. 1m E of Crichton Village; in the middle of a field. Access is gained through a short passage to a gallery about 50 ft long, 6 ft broad and about the same in height. The flat slabs of the original roof survive in places (the arched parts are modern) and, on one of the lintels near the end of the passage, the carving of the front half of a *Pegasus* or winged horse may still be seen. This stone and about 70 dressed blocks, some of which have diamond chisel-marks, are of Roman origin and must have been pillaged from a nearby Roman structure.

P.S.A.S., viii (1868–70), 105–9; lix (1924–5), 94–5; R.C.A.M.S. *Midlothian*, no. 61, p. 53–4.

DALMAHOY HILL

Fort

NT 135669; Sheet 62. 1½m W of Balerno.

The layout of this fort, in which a number of subsidiary enclosures cluster round a central and stronger citadel, has been compared to the Dark Age fort of Dunadd (Argyll). The summit fortification, 85 by 140 ft internally, has also been compared to the second phase at Craigie Hill (West Lothian).

P.S.A.S., lxxxiii (1948–9), 186–98; Feachem. 136–7

The nearby fort on Kaimes Hill (NT 130665) is systematically being destroyed by quarrying; for the most recent excavations see *Glasgow Archaeological Journal*, 1 1969), 7–28.

GLENCORSE CHURCH

Cup-and-Ring Marked Stone

NT 246626; Sheet 62.

A large boulder which has been moved to the outside of Glencorse Parish Church has been decorated with about twenty-two cups, some with faint rings, and 5 cup-and-ring markings with radial grooves.

R.C.A.M.S. *Midlothian*, no. 106, p. 76.

NEWBRIDGE

Cairn and Standing Stones

NT 123726; Sheet 62.

This cairn and series of standing stones occupies a position near the Newbridge roundabout on the

main Edinburgh–Glasgow road. The cairn is about 100 ft in diameter and 10 ft high and is surrounded by a modern wall. There are three stones round it (though they are not concentric); a fourth stone, 350 yds to E, may be an outlier of this setting.
R.C.A.M.S. *Midlothian*, no. 131, p. 95; Feachem, 81.

TORMAIN HILL

Cup-and-Ring Markings
NT 129696; Sheet 62. In the wood on top of the hill; on Bonnington Mains Farm, 3¼m SW of Ratho. There are eight expanses of rock outcrop decorated with cup-marks, cup-and-ring marks and grooves.
P.S.A.S., xvi (1881–2), 82–4; R.C.A.M.S. *Midlothian*, no. 223, p. 164.

PEEBLESSHIRE

BLACK MELDON

Fort
NT 206425; Sheet 62. 3m WNW of Peebles.
The stone-walled fort is situated on the summit of Black Meldon; it is 130 by 240 ft internally and on the W is additionally protected by a second wall.
R.C.A.M.S. *Peeblesshire*, no. 259, p. 101.

CADEMUIR HILL

Forts
NT 230373; 224370; Sheet 69. 2½m SW of Peebles.
The fort on the W ridge of the hill is a 5½ acre fort protected on all sides except the S by a stone wall and a rampart. There are the remains of about 35 hut platforms within the fort. The second fort at the SW end of the summit comprises a stone wall with both outer and inner facing-stones visible; a series of subsidiary terraces are also walled. The remains of a *cheveaux de frise* (stones set on end to impede access) are visible on the E side below the fort.
R.C.A.M.S. *Peeblesshire*, nos. 263–4, p. 102–5; Feachem, 141.

CASTLE HILL, HORSBURGH CASTLE FARM

Palisaded Settlement and Earthen Homestead
NT 291400; Sheet 62. 2½m ESE of Peebles.
Although neither site has survived completely, traces of both the earlier palisaded settlement and the later earthwork-enclosed homestead are clearly visible on the ground. Two concentric lines of double palisade enclosed a number of circular timber houses, and were subsequently overlain by double banks and ditches surrounding three timber-built houses.
R.C.A.M.S. *Peeblesshire*, no. 195, p. 74–5.

DREVA

Fort and Settlement
NT 126353 (fort); 127353 (settlement); Sheet 69.
This superb fort occupies the summit of Dreva Craig 200 yds from the by-road between Broughton and Stobo; two stone walls protect the highest part of the hill and the remains of four stone hut-foundations are visible in the interior. Below the fort on the SW there is a *cheveaux de frise* (as at Cademuir Hill), and between the road and the fort the ruined walls of a small settlement of uncertain date can be picked out. From this commanding position the sites of several other hill-forts can be seen.
R.C.A.M.S. *Peeblesshire*, no. 275, p. 111–4; Feachem, 143.

HAREHOPE

Homestead
NT 203448; Sheet 62. ½m NE of Harehope farm-house.
This site is particularly well-preserved and represents an unusual type of homestead; two major phases of construction are visible, each consisting of a double ring of substantial banks, the later ring set immediately within the earlier. Excavation has shown that these banks were crowned by sturdy timber fences, and traces of three superimposed wooden houses were found in the centre of the interior.
R.C.A.M.S. *Peeblesshire*, no. 199, p. 77; Feachem, 141–2.

HAREHOPE RINGS

Fort
NT 196445; Sheet 62. ½m NW of Harehope farm-house.
An attractive fort with twin ramparts and the re-mains of hut-platforms in the interior; a linear ditch impedes access from the NW.
R.C.A.M.S. *Peeblesshire*, no. 285, p. 118–20; Feachem, 142.

HARESTANES, KIRKURD

Stone Circle
NT 124443; Sheet 62. In a private garden 750 yds E of Harestanes farm.
This attractive circle of five stones has an internal diam. of 10 ft.
R.C.A.M.S. *Peeblesshire*, no. 107, p. 63; Feachem, 83–4.

LYNE

Roman Fort
NT 188405; Sheet 62. 4m W of Peebles.
Well-preserved remains of a fort built in the late Antonine period; the turf rampart is visible for almost the complete circuit (fig. 42).
R.C.A.M.S. *Peeblesshire*, no. 374, p. 171–5.

WHITESIDE HILL

Fort
NT 168461; Sheet 62. 1¼m SE of Romannobridge.
The impressive remains of this fort consist of nine visible house-platforms enclosed first by a single rampart and ditch and subsequently by multiple ramparts. Traces of annexes at the N and S ends of the fort represent probable stock-pens. An outlying linear earthwork bars access to the fort. A stone wall was built inside the abandoned defences possibly in the late or post-Roman periods (fig. 48).
R.C.A.M.S. *Peeblesshire*, no. 331, p. 152–3; Feachem, 142.

WHITE MELDON

Cairn, Fort, Unenclosed Platform Settlements

NT 219428 (cairn, fort); NT 216434, 218436 (platforms); Sheet 62.
The largest of the Peeblesshire forts occupies the summit of the White Meldon 2½m NW of Peebles; the remains of four lines of defence can be seen on the E side and in the interior there are several hut-platforms and a cairn (45 ft in diam. and 3 ft in height). On the W and NW flanks of the hill below the fort there are two unenclosed platform settle-ments each with nine platforms.
R.C.A.M.S. *Peeblesshire*, no. 67, p. 59 (cairn); nos. 192–3, p. 74 (unenclosed platform settlements); no. 330, p. 148–52 (fort); Feachem, 141.

PERTHSHIRE

Only chambered cairns are described here as these are not represented in other counties.

CLACH NA TIOMPAN

Chambered Cairn
NN 830330; Sheet 48. 6½m SW of Amulree.
The impressive remains of this cairn, aligned NW-SE, are close to the private road in the upper part of Glen Almond. The cairn is about 190 ft long and between 20 and 38 ft in breadth.
The remains of three *Clyde*-type chambers are still visible, the SE one being the best preserved (figs. 4 and 5).
P.S.A.S., lxxxviii (1954–6), 112–21; Feachem, 57.

KINDROCHAT

Chambered Cairn
NN 723229; Sheet 54. 3m W of Comrie
This cairn, standing in private ground, was ex-cavated in 1929–30; it measures about 135 ft long and 36 ft broad and is aligned E and W. The major chamber is at the E end and there are two side chambers on the S (fig. 4).
P.S.A.S., lxiv (1929–30), 264–72; lxv (1930–1), 281–93; Feachem, 57–8.

ROTTENREOCH

Chambered Cairn

NN 842206; Sheet 54. 2m SW of Crieff.
This ruined cairn measures about 50 ft by 190 ft; at the NE end are the remains of a *Clyde*-type chamber about 12 ft in length. At the SW end a series of upright slabs may be all that survives of another.
P.S.A.S., lxxvii (1942–3), 31–2; Feachem, 58.

CULTOQUHEY

Chambered Cairn
NN 892234; Sheet 55. 2m NE of Crieff; in the private grounds of Cultoquhey House.
The *Clyde*-type chamber is at the edge of a large natural mound; the chamber is 10 ft long and divided by a cross-slab into two compartments.
P.S.A.S., xcii (1958–9), 74.

ROXBURGHSHIRE

EILDON HILL NORTH

Fort and Roman Signal Station
NT 555328; Sheet 70. 1m SE of Melrose.
This fort occupies the NE summit of the Eildon Hills above the valley of the Tweed. The defences now most clearly visible belong to the final phase of construction; they enclose an area of some 40 acres, within which are about 300 platforms representing the sites of circular timber houses. Among these houses at the W end of the fort have been found the foundations of a timber-built Roman signal station, set within a penannular ditch.
R.C.A.M.S. *Roxburghshire*, no. 597, p. 306–10; Feachem, 150; *P.S.A.S.*, lxxxvi (1951–2), 202–5.

GREENBROUGH

Palisaded Homestead
NT 813169; Sheet 70. 2¼m SE of Hownam village.
This sub-rectangular homestead is situated on the flat summit of Greenbrough Hill, overlooking the valley of the Heatherhope Burn; the forts of Black-brough and Sundhope Kipp lie on adjacent hills on either side. The line of the enclosing palisade, its entrance on the NE and two circular houses within it are clearly visible as shallow grooves in the turf (fig. 27). The site measures approximately 95 by 75

ft, and the houses about 25 and 21 ft in diameter respectively.
R.C.A.M.S. *Roxburghshire*, no. 316, p. 175; Feachem, 98.

HAYHOPE KNOWE

Palisaded Settlement
NT 860176, Sheet 70. 5m ESE of Hownam village.
This settlement lies at a height of 1100 ft OD on a spur of the main Cheviot ridge, overlooking the Kelsocleuch Burn. Excavation revealed that the primary settlement of some dozen houses had been enclosed by a double palisade with an outer fence set at a distance of 20–40 ft. The interior measured 285 by 165 ft with two entrances, and the circular timber houses were between 36 and ·42 ft in diameter. The settlement was subsequently strengthened by the addition of a bank and ditch, but this work remained unfinished (fig. 28).
R.C.A.M.S. *Roxburghshire*, no. 665, p. 342–3; Feachem, 151; *P.S.A.S.*, lxxxiii (1948–9), 45–67.

HOWNAM RINGS

Palisade, Fort, Settlement and Homestead
NT 790194; Sheet 70. ½m E of Hownam village.
The remains of this complex site lie on a flat-topped hill above the Kale Water. The sequence uncovered by excavation comprises a palisaded enclosure, a fort enclosed first by a stone wall and later by four earthen and rubble ramparts, an open settlement of circular stone houses, and a sub-rectangular enclosure containing a single stone-walled house. The open settlement and the homestead were superimposed within and upon the abandoned fort defences.
R.C.A.M.S. *Roxburghshire*, no. 301, p. 160; Feachem, 151.

LONG KNOWE

Long Cairn
NY 527862; Sheet 76. 3m ESE of Newcastleton.
The cairn is about 175 ft long from N to S, 45 ft across, and still stands to a height of 5 ft. The slabs

visible on the surface may be the remains of cists which were examined in the 1860's.
R.C.A.M.S. *Roxburghshire*, no. 110, p. 94; Feachem, 58.

RUBERS LAW

Fort
NT 580155; Sheet 70. 5¼m SW of Jedburgh.
This fort occupies an imposing situation on an isolated hill rising to a height of almost 1400 ft OD above Teviotdale. The pre-Roman fort of about 7 acres was enclosed by a stone-faced rubble wall. A smaller fort containing a total area of about 600 by 200 ft was later built on the summit of the hill; since the walls of this fort incorporate much dressed masonry, it is assumed that a Roman signal station had been built on the hill and that this secondary fort is of late or post-Roman date.
R.C.A.M.S. *Roxburghshire*, no. 145, p. 102–5; Feachem, 153.

WODEN LAW

Fort and Roman Siege-Works
NT 768 125; Sheet 70. 4m S of Hownam village.
This fort stands on a prominent hill overlooking the valley of the Kale Water, at a height of almost 1400 ft OD (fig. 30). It consists of a primary stone wall, which was later replaced by two ramparts with a medial ditch. These ramparts were demolished soon after their construction and the fort was abandoned during the local Roman occupation. Subsequent native re-occupation is represented by a stone wall built within the original defences.
The abandoned fort was used by the Roman army for siege-practice. Two banks between three ditches were constructed to surround the fort at a distance of approximately 70 ft, just beyond the fatal range of a missile thrown by hand from the fort. In-complete lines of earthwork lie beyond this main siege-work. Woden Law is thought to have been a practice-ground for the troops stationed 1¼m away at the Pennymuir camps.
The Roman road known as Dere Street runs along the approach to Woden Law from Hunthall Hill and down the N flank of the Law; this section of the road, from Brownhart Law, SE of Woden Law,

to Whitton Edge, W of Hownam, is particularly well-preserved. A series of five cross-dykes spans the ridge between Woden Law and Hunthall Hill.
R.C.A.M.S. *Roxburghshire*, no. 308, p. 169–72; nos. 401–3, p. 192 (dykes); D. R. Wilson, *Roman Frontiers of Britain*, 1967, 74–5; Feachem, 152–3.

SELKIRKSHIRE

THE RINK

Fort
NT 480327; Sheet 69. 2½m S of Galashiels; ½m N of The Rink farm.
Impressive remains of a hill-fort stand within a plantation. Two ramparts with a ditch between are in a good state of preservation and have an overall diam. of some 200 ft. The single entrance is to the E.
R.C.A.M.S. *Selkirkshire*, no. 122, p. 92–3; Feachem, 155.

TORWOODLEE

Fort and Broch
NT 475384; Sheet 69. 2m NW of Galashiels; 580 yds N of Torwoodlee Mains farm. The fort, which originally measured 350 by 450 ft, is now only visible on the N and W. The broch, which is situated at the W side, has an internal diameter of 40 ft, with walls about 18 ft thick and up to 3 ft in height. Cells within the thickness of the walls.
P.S.A.S., lxxxv (1950–1), 92–117; R.C.A.M.S. *Selkirkshire*, no. 118, p. 88–91; Feachem, 154–5.

STIRLINGSHIRE

THE ANTONINE WALL

(Stirlingshire and West Lothian)
Sheet 61.
The Wall will be described from E to the W boundary of the region at Castlecary.
The E end was marked by an impressive carved slab or 'distance slab' at Bridgeness (now in N.M.A.); one panel portrays a ceremonial sacrifice, the other

the defeat of the native resistance (fig. 40), with a commemorative inscription between. The site of the fort at Carriden, just to the E of the end of the Wall, can be pinpointed from air photographs, but no surface traces survive (NT 025807), and the fort which probably existed at Kinneil can no longer be located. The position of the fort at Inveravon (NS 950796) has recently been discovered and confirmed by excavation.

The fort at Mumrills (NS 918794) cannot be seen on the surface but excavations in 1923–28 and 1960 have shown the plan of the fort and some of its internal features, including the headquarters building, officer's quarters and granaries as well as a bath house. The fort at Falkirk and the fortlet at Watling Lodge have now been destroyed, although the site of the latter is known.

Rough Castle (NS 843798), 2½m W of Falkirk, is the most impressive surviving fort and section of wall and ditch; these are in the care of the Department of the Environment. The fort is one acre in area and excavations revealed the central headquarters building round which were the barrack blocks. The stone foundations of a bath house were found in an annexe to the fort on the E side. An unusual additional defence on the N, beyond the wall, was a series of pits which originally held sharpened stakes, to impede approach from this side. Seabegs, its neighbour, has been completely obliterated, while Castlecary (NS 789782) has been cut through by the Edinburgh-Glasgow railway line. Its plan has been partly recovered by excavation and portions of its defences can still be detected on the ground.

Several stretches of the wall or the ditch survive, notably those in the care of the Department of the Environment at Watling Lodge, 1½m W of Falkirk (NS 862798), a good section of ditch showing its V-profile, and at Seabegs Wood, 1m SW of Bonnybridge (NS 813793), where both rampart and ditch survive and it is possible to pick out the Military Way. An impressive stretch of the Wall exists on either side of the fort of Rough Castle and includes two beacon-stances (or 'expansions') on either side of the fort, although that at Tentfield West (NS 850799) is not easy to see. The other three are Tentfield East (NS 855798) and Bonnyside East and West (NS 838798 and 834798).

Sir George Macdonald, *The Roman Wall in Scotland*, 1934. A. S. Robertson, *The Antonine Wall*, 1970. R.C.A.M.S. *Stirlingshire*, 32–6, 93–118. D. R. Wilson, *Roman Frontiers of Britain*, 1967. O.S. Period Map, *The Antonine Wall*, 1969.

CASTLETON

Cup-and-Ring Markings
NS 863880, 862883; Sheet 55. 2m W of Airth; 100 yds S of Castleton Farm and 160 yds NW of farm.
There are several areas of rock outcrop, decorated with cup-and-ring markings; some cups surrounded by five concentric rings.
P.S.A.S., c., (1967–8), 72–3.

CRAIGTON

Dun
NS 628872; Sheet 54. ¾m NE of Fintry; ¼m NW of Craigton Farm.
Apart from this and the site at Leckie (NS 693940), none of the Stirlingshire duns is at all well preserved. The outline of the dun at Craigton is still visible as a stony bank; several outer-facing stones survive, particularly on the NW. Two stretches of an outer defence are visible on the NW and SE.
R.C.A.M.S. *Stirlingshire*, no. 89, p. 82–3.

DUMYAT

Fort
NS 832973; Sheet 54. 2½m E of Bridge of Allan.
The fort occupies a shoulder of this hill at 1000 ft OD and the remains of two walls and a small circular fort (possibly secondary) can still be seen.
R.C.A.M.S. *Stirlingshire*, no. 68, p. 69–71; Feachem, 157.

DUNMORE

Fort
NS 605864; Sheet 54. On the top of Dunmore (1126 ft OD), ½m W of Fintry.
The major remains are those of a stone wall (12 ft thick) enclosing an area 170 by 530 ft; the scattered remains of a series of outworks can still be seen.
R.C.A.M.S. *Stirlingshire*, no. 77, p. 76–8.

HILL OF AIRTHREY (Fairy Knowe, Pendrich)

Cairn

NS 796981; Sheet 54. ½m N of Bridge of Allan; ¼m SE of Sunnylaw Farm.

This cairn still measures 60 ft in diameter and stands over 7 ft in height; it was excavated in 1868 when it was said to be 21 ft high. A Beaker was found as a secondary deposit some 2 ft from the top of the mound and a central cist covered by a small cairn contained six flint arrowheads (fig. 49).

R.C.A.M.S. *Stirlingshire*, no. 6, p. 59–60.

TAPPOCH BROCH, TOR WOOD

Broch

NS 833849; Sheet 61. 2¼m NW of Larbert; in the centre of Tor Wood (recently replanted).

The internal area measures 32 by 35 ft within a massive wall; the entrance passage survives intact with two lintel stones still in position. The broch has been excavated on several occasions and sherds of pottery, quern fragments and slabs with cup-and-ring markings have been discovered.

R.C.A.M.S. *Stirlingshire*, no. 100, p. 85–7; Feachem, 172.

CAIRNPAPPLE

Henge and Cairn

NS 987717; Sheet 61. 1¼m ESE of Torphichen.

This important site has been fully described in the text (fig. 10); it provides an excavated sequence illustrating the changes of ritual in the 2nd millennium B.C. The site is protected by the Department of the Environment and there is an attractive museum; a useful explanatory leaflet is on sale.

P.S.A.S., lxxxii (1947–8), 68–123.

CRAIGIE HILL

Fort

NT 154758; Sheet 62. 1m SE of Dalmeny.

The fort occupies the summit of a steep-sided ridge and measures 750 by 150 ft internally; the E side seems to rely on its natural defensive position but along the W are the remains of three walls, and within there is a series of hut platforms. There is a secondary stone-walled fort at the N end.

R.C.A.M.S. *West Lothian*, no. 327, p. 206–7; Feachem, 159.

Museums

National Museum of Antiquities of Scotland, Edinburgh

The majority of the prehistoric finds from the area have been deposited in the National Museum, which has good displays of representative material from all periods.

Hunterian Museum, University of Glasgow

Possesses prehistoric and Roman material from south-east Scotland.

Huntly House Museum, Canongate, Edinburgh

Contains the finds from the Roman fort at Cramond.

There are also local museums with smaller prehistoric sections at *Dunfermline, Hawick, Kirkcaldy, Peebles, Selkirk* and *Stirling*. There are collections which contain material from North Fife, Perthshire and Angus in the *Dundee Museum and Art Gallery* and *Perth Art Gallery and Museum*.

Select Bibliography

References for individual sites have been provided in the Gazetteer.

GENERAL

Geological information is provided by the Ordnance Survey *Geological Survey Ten-Mile Map*, 1957.

J. B. Sissons, *The Evolution of Scotland's Scenery*, 1967.

British Association for the Advancement of Science, *Scientific Survey of South-Eastern Scotland*, 1951; *Dundee and District*, 1968.

The complete region has been covered by the county Inventories of the Royal Commission on the Ancient and Historical Monuments of Scotland, *Berwickshire*, Revised Issue, 1915; *East Lothian*, 1924; *Midlothian and West Lothian*, 1929; *Fife, Kinross and Clackmannan*, 1933; *Roxburghshire*, 1956; *Selkirkshire*, 1957; *Stirlingshire*, 1963; *Peeblesshire*, 1967.

V. G. Childe, *The Prehistory of Scotland*, 1935.

R. Feachem, *A Guide to Prehistoric Scotland*, 1963.

S. Piggott (ed.) *The Prehistoric Peoples of Scotland*, 1962.

HUNTERS AND GATHERERS

J. G. Callander, 'A Collection of Tardenoisian Implements from Berwickshire', *P.S.A.S.*, lxi (1926–7), 318–27.

J. G. D. Clark, 'Notes on the Obanian with Special Reference to Antler- and Bone-work', *P.S.A.S.*, lxxxix (1955–6), 91–106.

A. D. Lacaille, *The Stone Age in Scotland*, 1954.

THE FIRST FARMERS

A. S. Henshall, *The Chambered Tombs of Scotland*, vol. i, 1963; vol. ii, forthcoming. 'The Long Cairns of Eastern Scotland', *Scottish Archaeological Forum*, (1970), 28–46.

I. J. McInnes, 'A Scottish Neolithic Pottery Sequence', *Scottish Archaeological Forum* (1969), 19–30.

S. Piggott, *The Neolithic Cultures of the British Isles*, 1954, reprinted 1970.

2000–600 B.C.

D. L. Clarke, *Beaker Pottery of Great Britain and Ireland*,' 1970.

J. M. Coles, 'Scottish Early Bronze Age Metalwork', *P.S.A.S.*, ci (1968–9), 1–110. 'Scottish Middle Bronze Age Metalwork', *P.S.A.S.*, xcvii (1963–4), 82–156. 'Scottish Late Bronze Age Metalwork: Typology, Distributions and Chronology', *P.S.A.S.*, xciii (1959–60), 16–134.

600 B.C.–A.D. 400

E. W. MacKie, 'Radiocarbon dates and the Scottish Iron Age', *Antiquity*, xliii (1969), 15–26.

C. M. Piggott, 'The excavations at Hownam Rings, Roxburgh, 1948', *P.S.A.S.*, lxxxii (1947–8), 193–225.

A. L. F. Rivet (ed.), *The Iron Age in Northern Britain*, 1966.

A. S. Robertson, 'Roman Finds from Non-Roman Sites in Scotland', *Britannia*, i (1970), 198–226.

A. Ross, *Everyday Life of the Pagan Celts,* 1970.

F. T. Wainwright (ed.), *The Problem of the Picts,* 1955.

ROMAN OCCUPATION

J. Curle, *A Roman Frontier Post and its People,* 1911.

Sir G. Macdonald, *The Roman Wall in Scotland,* 1934.

I. A. Richmond (ed.), *Roman and Native in North Britain,* 1958.

A. S. Robertson, *The Antonine Wall,* 1970.

THE VOTADINI

K. H. Jackson, *The Gododdin,* 1969.

Index